A CLASSIC RETELLING

MACBETH

by William Shakespeare

nextext

Printed in the United States of America.

ISBN 0-618-03147-2

1 2 3 4 5 6 7 — QKT — 06 05 04 03 02 01 00

Picture Acknowledements

Page 10, 16(background), 17 (inset and background), 18, 19, 26:
CORBIS/BETTMAN

Page 15: CORBIS

Page 16 (inset): CORBIS/Hulton-Deutsch Collection

Page 20: CORBIS/Chris Heller

Page 21: The British Library

Pages 23 & 25: from The Complete Works of Shakespeare, edited by David
Bevington. Copyright © 1997 by Addison-Wesley Educational Publishers Inc.
Reprinted by permission.

Table of Contents

ACT ONE

Macbeth. Malcolm tests Macduff and finds that he is sincere. Ross tells Macduff of his family's murder. Macduff swears to get revenge.

ACT FIVE

Vocabulary words appear in boldface type and are
footnoted. Specialized or technical words and phrases
appear in lightface type and are footnoted.

Background

William Shakespeare lived and wrote near the end of a time in European history known as the Renaissance, which lasted from 1485 to 1660. The voyages of Christopher Columbus and the Pilgrims' landing at Plymouth happened during the Renaissance. The word *renaissance* means "rebirth." During this time, there was a rebirth of interest in the arts and sciences of the classical Greeks and Romans. Some of Shakespeare's plays were based on classical stories. Others, like *Macbeth*, were based on history. Shakespeare often changed historical facts to make his plays more exciting.

Illustration Macbeth sees his mortal enemy.

The Story of *Macbeth*

Macbeth, a heroic Scottish general, lets his desire to become king corrupt him. Encouraged by the words of three witches and urged on by his wife, Macbeth murders Duncan, king of Scotland, and takes the throne. One murder leads to others. A hero destroys and is destroyed. This play is a tragedy because Macbeth has great qualities but his desire for power brings him down.

Shakespeare wrote this play for James I, who was king of England. In 1606, the king of Denmark came to visit his sister Anne, James's wife. James asked Shakespeare to write a play for the occasion.

Shakespeare wrote a play he knew James would like. James had also been king of Scotland, so Shakespeare chose a Scottish hero for his play and set it in Scotland. Many of the characters are James's ancestors. James had written about witches, so shakespeare gave witches an important role in the story. Shakespeare also knew that James often fell asleep or left early if a play was too long. Perhaps this is why *Macbeth* is Shakespeare's shortest serious play.

There is much witchcraft and magic in this play. Superstitious actors thought it was cursed. For this reason, it has become a tradition among actors never to say the play's name. They call it the Scottish Play.

▲

Theater of Shakespeare's time.

Shakespeare's Theater

The Globe theater was built in 1599 in a small town outside London called Southwark. It was an outdoor summer theater. In 1613, the theater burned down. It was rebuilt in 1614 but was torn down in 1644. However, in London today, Shakespeare's plays are performed in a newly built Globe theater. Now, as it was in Shakespeare's time, when the flag is flying over the Globe, a play is going on.

The Globe theater was round and had no roof. Its stage stuck out into the audience. As many as

2,000 people attended the plays, and most of them stood on the ground around the stage. Three audience balconies had seats that were covered. The most expensive seats were on the shady side.

The stage had doors on either side. There was a small curtain-covered room at the back of the stage and two balconies above it. The second balcony was for the musicians, whose music was like a soundtrack for the play. Above the stage was a ceiling painted to look like the sky. It was held up by two columns. Above the ceiling was a special effects room. Cannons were fired there for the battle scenes. Sound effects, like the screeching horses and roaring winds in this wild and gloomy play, were made in the special effects room.

The stage also had a trap door that could be used for magical appearances. There was constant activity in Shakespeare's theater. In *Macbeth*, the witches' cooking pot is set over the trap door so that the spirits they call up seem to rise from the pot. There was no additional scenery, except for a table or chair. The fast action of *Macbeth* was not slowed down by scene changes.

Shakespeare's Language

Poetry

Shakespeare wrote his plays in verse. Some of it does not rhyme and some of it does. The meter, or rhythm of the language, is what makes it poetry. Shakespeare's poetry is in ten-syllable lines with alternating stresses. This kind of verse is called "iambic pentameter." For example:

> *And often times, to win us to our harm,*
> *The instruments of darkness tell us truths.*

In this retelling, Shakespeare's poetry is not always used. However, some of his most famous lines have been. A note will tell you when the lines are exactly as Shakespeare wrote them.

Imagery

In Act Two, Scene Two, in a famous speech about sleep, Macbeth describes sleep "that knits up the ravell'd sleeve of care . . . balm of hurt minds, great nature's second course." He is using language to build up an image of healing. Shakespeare makes great use of imagery all through his plays.

Puns and Other Fun with Words

Shakespeare loved to have fun with language. He enjoyed jokes. He liked words and phrases that have more than one meaning. In the notes, *Wordplay* will point out some of these. Shakespeare's writing shows off the many meanings that a single statement can have. In Act Two, Scene Three of *Macbeth,* the drunken porter plays with words as he talks about drink. His speech is an example of Shakespeare's fun with words.

▲
Play Poster Early playbill for a Thos. W. Keene production of *Macbeth.*

The Characters

▲
Macbeth

The Major Characters

Duncan—King of Scotland

Malcolm—the king's older son

Donalbain—the king's younger son

Macbeth—Duncan's cousin, and a general in the Scottish army; later, thane of Cawdor and king of Scotland

Lady Macbeth—Macbeth's wife

Seyton—an officer attending Lady Macbeth

Lady—attending Lady Macbeth

Banquo—a thane of Scotland and a general in the Scottish army

Fleance—Banquo's son

Macduff—thane of Fife

Lady Macduff—Macduff's wife

Macduff's Son

Thanes and Noblemen of Scotland
    Lennox
    Ross
    Menteith
    Angus
    Caithness

Siward—Earl of Northumberland; commander of the English army, uncle to Malcolm and Donalbain

Young Siward—son of Siward

Illustration Lady Macbeth welcomes King Duncan and his men to the castle.

Lady Macbeth

Minor Characters

English Doctor
Scottish Doctor

Sergeant

Porter—opens the gates at
Macbeth's castle

Old Man

Three Murderers

Hecate—goddess of the evil
part of the night and the protector of witches

Three Witches

Three Apparitions—ghosts
and phantoms called up to
confuse Macbeth

Banquo's Ghost

Others:
    Lords
    Gentlemen
    Officers
    Soldiers
    Servants
    Attendants
    Messengers

The Plot

Act Three
Macbeth destroys anyone he considers to be a threat: his best friend, women, and even children.

Act Two
Macbeth, with the help of his wife, murders the king and becomes the new king.

Act One
On a gloomy, stormy night, three witches appear to Macbeth and Banquo. They suggest that Macbeth will become king.

Climax

Rising Action

Beginning

Illustration Lady Macbeth, sleepwalking, tries to rub the blood from her hands. A Lady and a Doctor watch.

Act Four

The witches plan to destroy Macbeth. They send false spirits that state—

- Macbeth must beware of Macduff.
- Macbeth cannot be defeated until Birnam Wood comes to Dunsinane Hill.
- Macbeth cannot be killed by any man born of woman.

Falling Action

Act Five

Macbeth feels safe because of the witches' predictions, but the witches' seemingly impossible statements come true, and Macbeth is killed.

End

William Shakespeare

Shakespeare's Life

Birth

Shakespeare was born in Stratford-upon-Avon, a small town about seventy-five miles northwest of London, England. His father, John Shakespeare, was a glove maker who owned a shop in Stratford and was elected to local government offices. Shakespeare's mother, Mary Arden, came from a farming family. Shakespeare was baptized on April 26, 1564, a few days after his birth. He was the third of eight children.

Childhood

Shakespeare went to school in Stratford. At this time, most people did not get an education and could neither read nor write. His school day was nine hours long. Shakespeare's education gave him the background for much of his writing. In fact, he took many of his ideas for his history plays from a common schoolbook of the time, Holinshed's *Chronicles*.

Stratford was an excellent place to grow up. The town was surrounded by woods, fields, and farms. It was a market town where people came to buy and sell goods. It was very busy, and Shakespeare had a chance to meet and observe many different types of people. During holidays,

COURTESY THE BRITISH LIBRARY

▲
Stratford

popular plays were performed. Traveling companies of actors visited the town, and there were two large fairs every year.

Marriage

In November 1582, at the age of eighteen, Shakespeare married Anne Hathaway, who was twenty-six. Their daughter Susanna was born in May 1583. Twins, Hamnet, a boy, and Judith, a girl, were born in 1585.

Queen Elizabeth I ▶

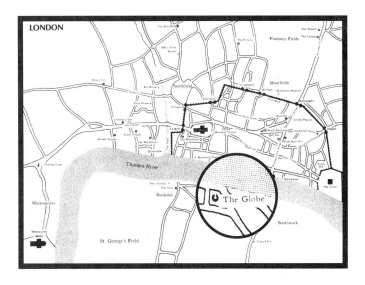

▲
Map of London

London

Seven years after the twins were born, Shakespeare was in London. He worked in the theaters—first in small jobs, then as an actor, and finally as a writer of plays. In 1599, he and six others became owners of the new Globe theater. Queen Elizabeth I supported Shakespeare's company. James I, who became king in 1603, gave the company a royal license. After that, it was known as the King's Men. The company often presented plays for the royal court.

Writing

Shakespeare's first plays were like those of another very popular author, Christopher Marlowe. As Shakespeare wrote more, he developed his own style. He wrote thirty-seven plays in all. His success came in part because he knew firsthand how audiences behaved and what they wanted. He gave audiences exciting stories. He provided funny moments in the midst of tragedies and tragic moments in the middle of comedies. He knew how easily audiences got bored and restless. He made sure there were surprises, magic events, songs, fights, love scenes, and jokes in all his plays.

The years 1592 to 1594 were times of much sickness and disease. The bubonic plague hit London then, and the theaters were often closed. Then Shakespeare turned to writing poems. He wrote two long, story-telling poems based on Greek mythology, *Venus and Adonis* (1593) and *The Rape of Lucrece* (1594). He also wrote a collection of 154 of the fourteen-line poems known as sonnets.

Later Years

Shakespeare's work brought him fame and money. In 1597, he bought himself a very large house called New Place in Stratford. He moved into it and began to spend more and more of his time there. His last play was *The Tempest,* in which a magician who has lived on a deserted magical island returns to his own land after he breaks his magical staff. Shakespeare seems to have gone on helping to write and fix other people's plays after he stopped writing his own. He died in 1616 and was buried in the church at Stratford.

▲
This is what New Place probably looked like during Shakespeare's ownership.

A Shakespeare Time Line

1564—William Shakespeare is baptized on April 26.

1582—He gets a license to marry Anne Hathaway in November.

1592—He is living in London. His first plays have been performed.

1592–1594—The bubonic plague spreads to London. Theaters close. Shakespeare turns to writing poetry.

1599—Shakespeare and six others buy the Globe theater.

1603—Queen Elizabeth I dies. The king of Scotland becomes James I of England.

1606—*Macbeth* is first performed.

1610—Shakespeare writes his last play, *The Tempest*.

1616—William Shakespeare dies on April 23.

ACT ONE, SCENE ONE

During a storm in a wild and deserted part of Scotland, three witches plot to meet with the Scottish general Macbeth, who is fighting an invading army.

[*Thunder and lightning. Enter three* Witches.]

First Witch. When shall we three meet again?
In thunder, lightning, or in rain?

Second Witch. When the hurlyburly's done.[1] When
the battle's lost and won.[2]

Third Witch. That will be before the set of sun.

First Witch. Where the place?

Second Witch. On the heath.[3]

---

[1] hurlyburly's done—uproar has stopped.

[2] How can a battle be lost and won? This is a *paradox*—something that seems impossible, but can be explained. Of course a battle can be lost and won. One side loses, and one side wins.

[3] heath—a deserted wasteland with small bushes and plants, but no trees.

Third Witch. There to meet with Macbeth.

First Witch. I come, Graymalkin.[4]

Second Witch. The toad calls.

Third Witch. Quickly!

All. Fair is foul, and foul is fair.[5] Fly through the
  fog and filthy air.

[*The* Witches *exit.*]

---

[4] She is talking to her cat Graymalkin. Cats and toads often
accompanied witches.

[5] This is another paradox—fair and foul (good and bad or beautiful and ugly)
are the opposites of each other, but the witches say they are the same.

*At King Duncan's camp near the battlefield, a wounded
sergeant reports that two generals, Macbeth and Banquo,
have beaten the invading Norwegians and some Scots who
were traitors. The king says he will make Macbeth the
thane[1] of Cawdor.*

[*A trumpet sounds offstage to announce the* King.]

[*Enter* King Duncan, *his two sons,* Malcolm *and*
Donalbain, Lennox, Lords[2] *and attendants for the
King, and a bleeding Sergeant.*]

Duncan. Who is this wounded man? From his
   looks he will be able to tell us how the battle
   is going.

---

[1] thane—a title for the six or so most important men in the kingdom next
to the king.

[2] Lords—members of the upper class who inherited their titles and power.
Together with the king and thanes, they ran the country.

Malcolm. This is the sergeant who saved my life today. Hail, brave friend! Tell the king how the fight was going when you left it.

Sergeant. No one could tell who was winning at first. The armies were like two tired swimmers who hang on to each other and almost drown themselves. The merciless Macdonwald, who went over to our enemy's side, had hired soldiers from the western islands.[3] Good fortune loved him. But that wasn't good enough. Brave Macbeth, well he deserves that name, with his sword cut a path until he reached the rebel Macdonwald. Macbeth didn't stop to shake hands or say good-bye before he ripped Macdonwald open from the navel to the jaw. Then Macbeth cut off Macdonwald's head and held it up on a spear!

Duncan. O brave cousin,[4] worthy gentleman!

Sergeant. And then, just as new storms and thunder come when the sun starts to shine, when we were feeling comfort, discomfort came. Listen, king of Scotland, listen. No sooner had Macbeth chased off the rebel's hired soldiers

---

[3] the western islands—The islands off the west coast of Scotland (the Hebrides).

[4] cousin—Macbeth is King Duncan's cousin. But in Shakespeare's time, the word *cousin* could mean any family member or even a close friend.

than the king of Norway, seeing his chance, attacked with new weapons and fresh men.

Duncan. Didn't this frighten our captains Macbeth and Banquo?

Sergeant. Yes, as sparrows make eagles afraid, or a rabbit makes a lion run. To tell the truth, I must report that Macbeth and Banquo were like cannons with double loads of gunpowder. So they doubled their fighting. Perhaps they were going to bathe in blood or make the place famous for death, I cannot tell.—But I am weak. My wounds need help.

Duncan. Your words and your wounds both tell of your courage. Go, find him doctors.

[*The* Sergeant *is helped off.*]

Duncan. Who is coming?

Malcolm. The worthy thane of Ross.

[*Enter* Ross *and* Angus.[5]]

Lennox. He is in a great hurry!

Ross. God save the king.[6]

---

[5] Shakespeare names several upper-class people in this play, but he doesn't make most of them very different from each other. The actors would have to do that.

[6] This was a normal way to greet the king.

Duncan. Where did you come from, worthy thane?

Ross. From Fife,[7] great king, where the Norwegians were killing our people. The king of Norway with a large army was helped by a traitor, the thane of Cawdor. They were winning until Macbeth, like the bridegroom of the goddess of war, joined the fight, hand to hand. And to end the story, we won.

Duncan. Great happiness!

Ross. And now the Norwegian king asks for peace terms. But Macbeth would not let the Norwegians bury their men until the king of Norway gave him ten thousand dollars, which Macbeth gave to our soldiers.

Duncan. The traitor thane of Cawdor won't trick us again. Go, have him executed, and give his title to Macbeth.

Ross. I'll see it done.

Duncan. What the traitor thane of Cawdor has lost, noble Macbeth has won.

[*They exit.*]

---

[7] Fife—a county in southeastern Scotland, near the capital of Edinburgh. Shakespeare's geography isn't always accurate in this play.

ACT ONE, SCENE THREE

In a bare, windy place near the battlefield, the witches show their magical powers. They predict Macbeth will be thane of Cawdor and king. They say Banquo will be the father of kings. Word comes that Macbeth is the new thane of Cawdor.

[*Thunder. Enter the three* Witches.]

First Witch. Where have you been, sister?

Second Witch. Killing pigs.

Third Witch. Sister, where have you been?

First Witch. A sailor's wife had chestnuts. She ate and ate and ate. "Give them to me," I said. "Get out of here, you witch," the fat, ugly woman cried. Her husband sailed to Aleppo.[1] He's the

---

[1] Aleppo—a city in the Middle East.

captain of the ship. But, in a **sieve**[2] I'll sail there, and like a rat without a tail I'll cause trouble for him.

Second Witch. I'll give you a wind to blow you there faster.

First Witch. You are kind.

Third Witch. And I'll give you another wind.

First Witch. I have all the other winds that blow from every direction on the compass. I'll drain him dry as hay. Sleep will not close his eyelids night or day. He shall live a man unable to sleep for nine times nine weeks, and he shall get weaker and sadder. Though his ship cannot be lost, yet it shall be storm-tossed. Look what I have.

[*The* Witch *shows a cut-off thumb.*]

Second Witch. Show me, show me.

First Witch. Here I have the thumb of a ship's pilot who was wrecked as he came home.[3]

[*A drum is heard offstage.*]

---

[2] **sieve**—a kitchen bowl with holes in it that is used to strain liquids. You wouldn't think anyone could sail in a sieve, but the witches are magic and supposedly could not drown.

[3] Witches used body parts to make their magic brews. A body part from a person who died violently was supposed to be the best.

Third Witch. A drum! A drum! Macbeth does come.

[*The* Witches *start to dance in a circle and chant.*]

All. The Weird Sisters,[4] hand in hand, messengers of the sea and land, thus do dance about, about. Three times to thine and three times to mine and three times again to make up nine.[5] Peace, the spell's made up.

[*Enter* Macbeth *and* Banquo.]

Macbeth. So foul and fair[6] a day I have not seen before.

Banquo. How far is it to the king's castle at Forres?

[Banquo *sees the* Witches. *He is not even sure if they are alive.*]

Banquo. What are these, so **withered**[7] and dressed so wildly? They don't look like anything that lives on the Earth, and yet they're on it. [*To the* Witches] Are you alive? Can you answer me?

---

[4] Weird Sisters—fate, sometimes shown as three women.

[5] The witches are making a magic spell. They are using magical numbers, like three.

[6] So foul and fair—almost repeats what the witches said at the end of their first scene. It is a paradox. How can a day be both fair and foul? Fair because they won. Foul because of the storm.

[7] **withered**—wrinkled and dried-up.

[*Each* Witch *puts a finger up to her lips, telling* Banquo *to be quiet.*]

Banquo. You seem to understand me, as each of you put your chapped fingers on your skinny lips. You should be women, but you have beards.

Macbeth. Speak if you can. What are you?

First Witch. All hail, Macbeth! Hail to thee, thane of Glamis![8]

Second Witch. All hail, Macbeth! Hail to thee, thane of Cawdor!

Third Witch. All hail, Macbeth, that shall be king hereafter.

[Macbeth *is very surprised by these greetings. He even jumps at the* Witches' *words.*]

Banquo. [*To* Macbeth] Good sir, why do you jump in fear when you hear things that sound so good? [*To the* Witches] Tell me the truth. Are you a dream or are you real? You greet my noble friend with good news of his present honor and suggestions of having a new title

---

[8] thane of Glamis—the title Macbeth inherited at his father's death. But Macbeth is surprised. How do these strange women know him? The next greeting is even more surprising. The witches greet Macbeth as thane of Cawdor. How do the witches know this? Macbeth doesn't know it yet. The witches' last greeting is most surprising: They say he will be king.

and becoming king. He seems **rapt**[9] with it. You haven't said anything to me. If you can see the future and say what will happen and what won't, speak to me. I don't beg you, and I don't fear you.

First Witch. Hail!

Second Witch. Hail!

Third Witch. Hail!

First Witch. Lesser than Macbeth and greater.

Second Witch. Not so happy, yet much happier.

Third Witch. You shall be the father of kings, but you will not be king. So all hail Macbeth and Banquo!

First Witch. Banquo and Macbeth, all hail!

Macbeth. Stop, you have not told me everything. Tell me more. Because of my father's death I know I am thane of Glamis. But how am I the thane of Cawdor? The thane of Cawdor is still alive and is honored,[10] and I can't believe I could be king any more than I could be the

---

[9] **rapt**—so carried away that he is not paying attention. But "rapt" sounds like "wrapped." Macbeth is wrapped in his cloak. This is the clothing or covering theme that runs through the play.

[10] Even though Macbeth beat the thane of Cawdor's army in battle, obviously Macbeth does not know that the thane of Cawdor was a traitor. Probably the thane of Cawdor did not lead his troops into battle.

thane of Cawdor.[11] Tell me how you know this and why you stop us in this deserted place with these greetings that seem to tell the future. Speak, I command you.

[*The* Witches *vanish.*]

Banquo. Water has bubbles, and it seems that earth has bubbles too. They have vanished like bubbles. Where are they?

Macbeth. They vanished into the air. They seemed real, but they vanished as your breath vanishes in the wind. I wish they had stayed!

Banquo. Were they really here? Or was this a dream?

Macbeth. Your children will be kings.

Banquo. You will be king.

Macbeth. And thane of Cawdor too. Isn't that what they said?

Banquo. Those exact words. [*Enter* Ross *and* Angus, *the messengers sent by the King.*] Who's here?

Ross. Macbeth, the king has happily heard of your

---

[11] This is dramatic irony—the audience or reader knows something that the character doesn't know. We know that Macbeth has already been named thane of Cawdor.

success. And, when he heard what you did in the fight, he could not praise you enough. Looking at what happened this day, he heard you were always in the middle of the worst fighting and never afraid of the death you made. Faster than they could be counted came message after message, and every one told the king how great you were in defending our country.

Angus. We are sent by the king to thank you. We are to bring you to the king, not reward you.

Ross. And as a promise of a greater honor, the king told me to call you thane of Cawdor. Hail, most worthy thane. For this title is yours now.[12]

Banquo. [*To himself*] What, can the devil[13] speak the truth?

Macbeth. The thane of Cawdor is alive. Why do you dress me in borrowed robes?[14]

Angus. The old thane of Cawdor is still alive, but will die for being a traitor. He helped Norway

---

[12] Macbeth is very surprised. The witches said he would be the thane of Cawdor, and right away he is. But Ross said this is just a "promise of a greater honor." There is only one thing greater than being a thane, being king.

[13] devil—refers to the witches.

[14] dress me in borrowed robes—robes are clothes, but here they stand for the thane of Cawdor's title and honors.

in this war, with money, troops, or information. He worked to ruin our country. By law, traitors must die. He has confessed. It has been proven. He is overthrown.

Macbeth. [*To himself*] I am Glamis, and now I am thane of Cawdor. The greatest prediction is still to come. [*To* Ross *and* Angus] Thanks for your pains. [**Aside**[15] *to* Banquo] Don't you hope your children will be kings now that we see this come true?

Banquo. If we can take this seriously, you might become the king. But it's strange. Often the instruments of darkness[16] tell us a small truth and win us with honest trifles[17] so that we will believe them, then they betray us in something important. [*To* Ross *and* Angus] Cousins, let me speak with you.

[Ross, Angus, *and* Banquo *step to the side to talk.*]

Macbeth. [*To himself*] Two truths are told that lead to my becoming king. [*To* Ross *and* Angus]

---

[15] **Aside**—a stage direction. It means that the actor should seem to be whispering to another character or thinking out loud to himself.

[16] darkness—evil.

[17] trifles—unimportant things.

I thank you, gentlemen. [*To himself*] This witches' promise cannot be bad, cannot be good. If it's bad, why has it given me a promise of success starting with a truth? I am thane of Cawdor. If it's good, why do I see a picture in my mind that makes my hair stand on end and my heart knock against my ribs? My fears are just horrible imaginings. My thought of murdering Duncan[18] is just a fantasy, and yet it shakes me so that it is all I can think about. Nothing is but what is not.[19]

Banquo. [*To* Ross *and* Angus] Look how our friend is rapt.

Macbeth. [*To himself*] If chance will make me king, why, chance may crown me without my doing anything.

Banquo. [*To* Ross *and* Angus] This new honor is like new clothes for Macbeth. He has to wear them for a while before they feel right.

Macbeth. [*To himself*] Come what will, even the roughest day passes.

---

[18] Macbeth sees that the fastest way for him to be king would be to get rid of Duncan. If he weren't caught, Macbeth would be the popular choice for king. He has just saved his country. He gave a large cash gift to the soldiers. He controls two thanedoms.

[19] Nothing seems real but the thought of murdering Duncan, which is just a fantasy.

Banquo. Worthy Macbeth, we are waiting for you.

Macbeth. I'm sorry. My dull brain was filled with things forgotten. Kind gentlemen, your pains are written where every day I turn the page to see them. Let us go to the king. [*To* Banquo] Think about what has happened, and when we have more time, let us speak freely to each other.

Banquo. Very gladly.

Macbeth. Till then, enough.—Come, friends.

[*They exit.*]

In a room in the king's palace, King Duncan rewards Macbeth but not Banquo. Duncan names his older son, Malcolm, as the next king. Duncan plans to visit Macbeth's castle.

[*Trumpets sound. Enter* King Duncan, Lennox, Malcolm, Donalbain, *and court* Attendants.]

Duncan. Has the old thane of Cawdor been executed?

Malcolm. My king, I have spoken with a man who saw him die. He very openly confessed his treason, asked your highness's pardon, and was deeply sorry. Nothing in his life became him like the leaving it. He died as if he had studied how to die. He threw away his life as if it were nothing.

Duncan. There's no way to find what someone is thinking by looking at his face. He was a gentleman whom I trusted totally.[1]

[*Enter* Macbeth, Banquo, Ross, *and* Angus.]

Duncan. O worthiest cousin, even now I was worried about not being able to thank you enough. What you have done is so great that I cannot thank you too much. I wish you had done less, so I could thank you more than you deserve. All I can say is you deserve more than I can give you if I gave you everything.

Macbeth. I owe you service and loyalty. Your highness's part is to accept my duty. My duty is to your throne and the country. We, your subjects, owe you what children owe their parents and servants owe their masters. We do what we should by doing everything to protect your love and honor.

Duncan. Welcome here. I have planted you and will work to make you grow even bigger. [*The* king *turns to* Banquo.] Noble Banquo, you have deserved as much as Macbeth, and everyone must know this. Let me hold you to my heart.

---

[1] Duncan's weakness is that he cannot judge people correctly.

[*The* king *hugs* Banquo.][2]

Banquo. There, if I grow, the harvest is yours.

Duncan. My great joys are causing me to weep. [Duncan *addresses everyone*] Sons, kinsmen, thanes, everyone, I am naming the next king, my oldest son, Malcolm. I name him the Prince of Cumberland,[3] and I will honor others as well. Let us now go from here to Macbeth's castle at Inverness and further honor Macbeth.

Macbeth. This is a great joy. I'll ride ahead and make my wife happy by telling her you're coming. I humbly take my leave.

Duncan. My worthy Cawdor.

Macbeth. [*To himself*] The Prince of Cumberland! That is a step that I must leap over or fall down. It is in my way. Stars, hide your fires; let not light see my black and deep desires.[4] Let my eye not see what my hand does, but let what my eye fears be done.

[Macbeth *exits.*]

---

[2] The king gave Macbeth a thanedom; he gives Banquo a hug. Kings were expected to reward those who helped them. This isn't much of a reward for Banquo.

[3] The Prince of Cumberland was heir to the throne. Since the king's son is much younger than Macbeth, if Macbeth wishes to become king, he will no longer just be able to wait until the old king dies.

[4] Throughout the play, light stands for good and dark for evil.

Duncan. True and worthy Banquo, Macbeth is brave, and praising him feeds me; it is a banquet to me. Let's follow Macbeth who has gone ahead to prepare to welcome us. He is the best kinsman.

[*Trumpets sound, and they exit.*]

In Macbeth's castle, Lady Macbeth reads a letter from Macbeth telling her what has happened. A messenger brings her news that the king is coming. Lady Macbeth urges Macbeth to look innocent and leave the rest to her.

[*Enter* Lady Macbeth, *reading a letter Macbeth wrote to her after he became thane of Cawdor.*]

Lady Macbeth. "The Weird Sisters met me after we won the battle, and I have learned without a doubt that they know more than people can know. When I tried to question them, they made themselves into air and vanished. While I stood amazed, two messengers came from the King and called me thane of Cawdor, which is the title the Weird Sisters called me and then said that in time I would be king. I wanted you to know this, my dearest partner of greatness, so you could rejoice in what is promised us. Keep it secretly in your heart, and farewell."

[*To herself*[1]] Glamis you are, and Cawdor, and shall be what you are promised. But I fear your nature; it is too full of the milk of human kindness to take the quickest way. You want to be great, are not without **ambition**,[2] but you do not have the cold heart that ambition needs. What you want, you want to get without doing wrong, and yet you would wrongly get it. You need to have, great Glamis, that which cries "You must do this," if you would have it. You fear to do what you would not have undone.[3] Come here quickly, so I may pour my spirit in your ear and punish with the bravery of my words all that keeps you from the golden crown that fate and magic seem to have you wearing already.

[*Enter a* Messenger.]

Lady Macbeth. What is your news?

Messenger. The king comes here tonight.

---

[1] This is a *soliloquy*, a long speech in which the character is thinking out loud.

[2] **ambition**—a strong wish to have power.

[3] Throughout the play, Macbeth and Lady Macbeth try to hide their evil even in their talk, so they almost never mention the murder. In this modern-language version, the murder is mentioned to make the action clearer.

Lady Macbeth. You are mad to say that. Isn't your master with him, who would send a message if the king were coming, so we could prepare?

Messenger. So please you, it is true. Our thane is coming. Another messenger was just ahead of him. That messenger had only enough breath to say the king is coming.

Lady Macbeth. Take care of him. He brings great news.

[*The* Messenger *exits.*]

Lady Macbeth. The **raven**[4] himself is hoarse that croaks the fatal entrance of Duncan into my castle. [Lady Macbeth *calls on the evil spirits.*] Come, you spirits that hear men's secret thoughts, remove my womanness and fill me from the head to the toe top-full of dreadful cruelty. Stop up the flow of natural kind feelings that might move me from my plan. Fill me full of bitterness, you who encourage murder, wherever you are waiting to do evil. Come, thick night, and cover me with the darkest smoke of hell so my knife cannot see the wound it makes, or heaven peep through the blanket of the dark to cry, "Stop, Stop!"

---

[4] **raven**—a large black bird with a very ugly croaking call. In myths, ravens could often talk and were a sign that something evil would happen.

[*Enter* Macbeth.]

Lady Macbeth. Great Glamis, worthy Cawdor, greater than both by the greeting to come! Your letter has taken me beyond the present, and I see the future.

Macbeth. My dearest love, Duncan comes here tonight.

Lady Macbeth. And when does he leave?

Macbeth. Tomorrow. He plans to leave tomorrow.

Lady Macbeth. O, never shall the sun see the tomorrow when Duncan leaves our castle![5]

[Macbeth *is startled that* Lady Macbeth *is so quickly planning to kill* Duncan.]

Lady Macbeth. Your face, my thane, is a book where men may read strange things. To deceive people, act normally. Carry welcome in your eye, your hand, your tongue. Look like the innocent flower, but be the poisonous snake under it. He that's coming must be taken care of. You shall put tonight's great business into my hands, which in all the nights and days to come will give us complete power.

---

[5] Lady Macbeth is saying that Duncan will never leave the castle.

Macbeth. We will speak more.

Lady Macbeth. Only look innocent. To look afraid
   is to be afraid. Leave all the rest to me.

[*They exit.*]

ACT ONE, SCENE SIX

In front of the castle, King Duncan arrives. Lady Macbeth welcomes him.

[*Musicians are playing. Torches are burning. Enter* King Duncan, Malcolm, Donalbain, Banquo, Lennox, Macduff,[1] Ross, Angus, *and court attendants.*]

Duncan. This castle is in a pleasant place. The air is sweet.

Banquo. The summer guest, the swallow, which often builds its nest on churches, lives here. Where these birds live, I have noticed, the air is sweet and healthy.

[*Enter* Lady Macbeth.]

---

[1] This is Macduff's first entrance. He doesn't speak. He will eventually be the *antagonist*, the person who stands up to the *protagonist* or main character.

Duncan. See, see our honored hostess! [*To* Lady Macbeth] All of these that love us[2] and travel with us are sometimes trouble, but we still thank them for their love. I say this to teach you to thank me for the trouble I am causing you by coming here, but I am here because I love you and your husband.

Lady Macbeth. Everything we can do, or twice do, or double that, would be poor in comparison to what you have given us. For all you have done for us in the past and the new honors you have given us, we are your servants.

Duncan. Where's the thane of Cawdor? We were right behind him and hoped to pass him, but he rides well, and his love for you has helped him to get to his home before us. Fair and noble hostess, we are your guest tonight.

Lady Macbeth. Your servants always have their own servants, and what is theirs they are ready to give to your highness, whenever you ask, to return what you have given them.

Duncan. Give me your hand.

[*He takes her hand.*]

---

[2] us—King Duncan is using the royal plural. Kings referred to themselves as if they were more than one person because they represented the whole country.

Duncan. Take me to my host. We love him highly and shall continue our favors to him. By your leave, hostess.

[*They exit.*]

In the castle, a party is held in the king's honor. Macbeth tells Lady Macbeth that he will not murder Duncan. Lady Macbeth persuades him to go on and explains her plan to kill Duncan.

[*Musicians. Torches.* Servants *enter carrying trays. There is a party going on offstage. Enter* Macbeth.]

Macbeth. If it[1] were finished when it's done, then it should be done quickly. If the crime could stop the punishment and I could be successful with his death, if this blow might be the end of it, then here in this place and time I wouldn't worry about God's judgment. But, in these cases, we still have judgment here. If we murder, we teach others how to murder. This

---

[1] it—the murder.

bloody instruction may return to torture us. If I murder him with a poisoned drink, then someone may poison me. Duncan is here because he trusts me for two reasons. First, I am his kinsman and his subject, both strong arguments against the deed. Then, I am his host. I should shut the door on his murderers, not use the knife myself. Besides, Duncan has used his powers so kindly, has been such a good king, that his virtues will plead like angels against the deep damnation of his murder. And, pity, like a naked newborn baby walking through a storm, or like heaven's messenger riding upon the winds, will blow the horrid deed in every eye so that tears will drown the wind. I have no spur to make my plan run faster, but only vaulting ambition, which jumps up on a horse and then falls back down on the other side.[2]

[*Enter* Lady Macbeth.]

Macbeth. How are things now, what news?

Lady Macbeth. He has almost finished eating. Why have you left the room?

---

[2] In this speech, Macbeth is struggling with two sides of himself—the honorable side and the ambitious side.

Macbeth. Has he asked for me?

Lady Macbeth. Don't you know he has?

Macbeth. We will go no further in this business.[3] He has honored me, and I have acquired golden opinions from all sorts of people, which should be worn now when they are new, not thrown away so soon.

Lady Macbeth. Was your hope drunk when you dressed yourself in it? Has it slept since? And does it wake now looking green and pale at what it planned to do? From this time I know you don't really love me. Are you afraid to do what you want to do? Would you have that which you think of as the greatest ornament[4] in life? Or would you live a coward in your own mind, like the poor cat in the story, saying "I dare not" instead of "I will"?[5]

Macbeth. I tell you—be quiet. I dare to do all that a man should do. There is no man who dares to do more.

---

[3] Macbeth says he will not kill Duncan. His better side has won—for the moment.

[4] the greatest ornament—the crown; being king.

[5] In the children's story, the cat wanted a fish from a pool of water, but didn't want to get its paws wet.

Lady Macbeth. Were you a beast when you told me you would do it? When you dared to do it, then you were a man. And you would be so much more of a man, if you would do it. You didn't have a time or place to do it then, and yet you would make a time and place. The time and place have made themselves, and their readiness unmakes you. I have nursed a baby and know how tender it is to love that baby. I would while it was smiling in my face pull my breast from its toothless gums and dash its brains out on a wall before I would break such a promise as you have made to me.

Macbeth. If we should fail?

Lady Macbeth. We fail? Screw your courage to the sticking place, and we'll not fail. [Lady Macbeth *starts the plan for murdering* King Duncan.] When Duncan is asleep, and this long journey will make him sleep, I will give his guards enough wine and beer to make them pass out. When they are in swinish[6] sleep, we can do what we wish to Duncan. We can then blame his guards for this great murder.

Macbeth. Have men children only, for your spirit

---

[6] swinish—piglike.

should make nothing but males. Will it not be believed—if we smear the sleeping guards with Duncan's blood and use their own daggers—that they had done it?

Lady Macbeth. Who would dare to say it any other way? We will cry and make a great noise at his death.

Macbeth. I have decided and will use all the power in me to do this terrible act. Away, and mock the time with fairest show.[7] False face must hide what the false heart does know.

[*They exit.*]

---

[7] show—expression on the face.

ACT TWO, SCENE ONE

In the castle, Macbeth meets Banquo and his son Fleance after the party. Macbeth prepares to murder the king. Macbeth believes he sees a dagger floating in the air that leads him to Duncan's room.

[*Enter* Banquo *and* Fleance, *who is carrying a torch.*[1] *It is well past midnight. The party has just ended.*]

Banquo. What time is it, boy?

Fleance. The moon is down. I have not heard the clock.

Banquo. The moon goes down at twelve.

Fleance. It must be later then, sir.

Banquo. Here, take my sword. [Banquo *gives his sword to* Fleance.] There's a good housekeeper

---

[1] torch—a light made from a burning stick of wood.

in heaven. They have put the candles[2] out. Take this too. [Banquo *hands something else to his son, perhaps his cape or his dagger.*] I am very sleepy, and yet I would not sleep. Merciful powers, hold back the cursed thoughts that come to me when I rest.

[*Enter* Macbeth, *and a* Servant *carrying a torch.*]

Banquo. [*To* Fleance] Give me my sword. [*To the people entering the stage*] Who's there?

Macbeth. A friend.

Banquo. What, sir, not yet at rest? The king's in bed. He is very happy, and has sent great gifts to you. This diamond he gives to your wife and calls her a most kind hostess. He went to bed very contented.

[*He gives* Macbeth *the diamond.*]

Macbeth. We were unprepared for the king, or we would have done better.

Banquo. All's well. I dreamed about the Weird Sisters last night. To you they have showed some truth.

---

[2] the candles—the stars and moon. They cannot see the stars. It must be getting near dawn.

Macbeth. I don't think about them. Yet, when we can find some time, I would like to speak to you about them.

Banquo. Whenever you will have the kindness to find time.

Macbeth. If you will support me when the right time comes, you shall gain honor.

Banquo. Just so I don't lose any honor in trying to gain honor. My conscience must be free of guilt and my loyalties clear. If so, I will listen to you and do what you say.

Macbeth. I hope you sleep well.

Banquo. Thanks, sir. The like to you!

[Banquo *and* Fleance *exit.*]

Macbeth. [*To the* Servant] Go tell Lady Macbeth that when my drink is ready, she should ring the small bell.[3] Then, get to bed. [*The* Servant *exits*]

[Macbeth *believes he sees a dagger floating in the air in front of him.*]

---

[3] When Lady Macbeth rings the bell, it will be a signal that the king's guards are drunk.

Macbeth. Is this a dagger which I see before me, the handle turned toward my hand? Come, let me hold you.

[Macbeth *reaches for the dagger.*]

I don't have you, and yet I see you still. Can't I feel you as well as see you, fatal vision? Or are you just a dagger of the mind, a false creation coming from my too excited brain?

[Macbeth *turns away and then looks back.*]

I see you still, in form as real as this dagger which now I draw.

[Macbeth *draws his dagger.*]

You lead me toward the way I was going, and suggest the weapon I was to use. My eyes are made fools by the other senses, or else worth all the rest.

[Macbeth *looks away, but when he looks at the dagger again, he sees blood on it.*]

I see you still, and on your blade and handle is blood that was not there before. There's no such thing. It is the bloody business that makes me see this.

[Macbeth *must calm himself and get back into the mood to murder.*]

Now over half the world it is night, and nature seems dead. Wicked dreams worry eyes closed in sleep. Witchcraft gives offerings to the goddess Hecate.[4] Withered murder is alarmed by his watchman, the wolf, whose howls announce the time. Thus murder with his quiet steps, like the raping Roman emperor Tarquin, moves like a ghost. You real and firm earth, hear not my steps for fear your very stones make noises that will tell where I am and take away the silent horror from the time which now seems so right. [Macbeth *realizes that he is wasting time.*] While I threaten, he lives. Too much talking keeps me from acting.

[*Offstage* Lady Macbeth *rings the bell that signals it's time to murder* Duncan.]

Macbeth. I go, and it is done. The bell invites me. Hear it not, Duncan, for it is a knell[5] That summons thee to heaven or to hell.[6]

[Macbeth *exits to kill* King Duncan.]

---

[4] Hecate—goddess of the evil part of night and protector of witches.

[5] knell—a bell rung slowly for a death or funeral.

[6] These three lines are Shakespeare's own ending to this famous scene.

In the castle, Macbeth and Lady Macbeth meet after the murder. Macbeth has forgotten to leave the daggers beside the murdered king. Lady Macbeth returns the daggers, making it look as if Duncan's guards have murdered him. There is a loud knocking at the front gate.

[*Enter* Lady Macbeth. *She is talking about the king's bodyguards.*]

Lady Macbeth. The wine that has made them drunk has made me brave. It has put them out, but given me fire. Hark![1] Peace. It was the owl that shrieked, the deadly town crier[2] that gives a frightening good night. He is doing it. The doors are open, and the drunken guards make a joke of their job by snoring. I have drugged their drinks. I don't know if they will live or die.

---

[1] Hark—listen. Lady Macbeth thinks she hears something. She knows Macbeth is murdering the king.

[2] The hoot of the owl foretells death.

Macbeth. [*Offstage*] Who's there? What's happening?

Lady Macbeth. [*To herself*] I am afraid they woke up, and it is not done. The attempt and not the deed has caught us. Hark! I laid their daggers ready; he could not miss them. If Duncan had not looked like my father as he slept, I would have killed him.[3]

[*Enter* Macbeth, *carrying the guards' bloody daggers.*]

Lady Macbeth. My husband?

Macbeth. I have done the deed. Did you hear a noise?

Lady Macbeth. I heard the owl scream and the crickets cry. Didn't you speak?

Macbeth. When?

Lady Macbeth. Now.

Macbeth. As I came down?

Lady Macbeth. Yes.

Macbeth. Hark! Who sleeps in the next room?

Lady Macbeth. The king's son, Donalbain.

---

[3] Lady Macbeth talked bravely before the murder. She thinks she should have murdered the king. But the sleeping king looked like her father, and she found she couldn't kill him.

[Macbeth *looks at his blood-covered hands.*]

Macbeth. This is a sorry sight.

Lady Macbeth. A foolish thought, to say a sorry sight.

Macbeth. One of the guards laughed in his sleep, and the other cried "Murder!" They woke each other. I stood and heard them. But they said their prayers and went back to sleep.

Lady Macbeth. There are two of them.

Macbeth. One cried "God bless us," and the other said "Amen," as if they had seen me with these bloody hands. I could not say "Amen" when they did say "God bless us."

Lady Macbeth. Don't worry so much about it.

Macbeth. But why couldn't I say "Amen"? I had a great need for a blessing, and "Amen"[4] stuck in my throat.

Lady Macbeth. These deeds must not be thought about in this way; it will make us mad.

---

[4] Macbeth couldn't pray because he had killed the king. During this time, Europeans saw the world as a great chain. God was at the top. The king was the next link. Everything and everyone was somewhere on the chain. But by killing the king, Macbeth has broken the chain. So, all the world is broken off from God, and especially, Macbeth is broken off from God.

Macbeth. I thought I heard a voice cry "Sleep
    no more!
  Macbeth does murder sleep,"—
    the innocent sleep,
  Sleep that knits up the ravell'd sleeve of care,
  The death of each day's life, sore labor's bath,
  Balm of hurt minds, great nature's second
    course,
  Chief nourisher in life's feast.[5]

Lady Macbeth. What do you mean?

Macbeth. Still it cried to all the house, "Sleep
no more! Glamis has murdered sleep, and
therefore Cawdor shall sleep no more. Macbeth
shall sleep no more."

Lady Macbeth. Who was it that cried this? Why,
worthy thane, you weaken your noble strength
to think so madly. Go get some water and wash
this blood from your hands.

[Lady Macbeth *suddenly sees the daggers that should
have been left with the sleeping guards to make them
look guilty.*]

Lady Macbeth. Why did you bring these daggers
from the place? They must lie there. Go, carry

---

[5] These famous six lines are in Shakespeare's original words: "ravell'd" means
twisted stitches in a piece of knitting. "Balm" is a healing ointment.

them back and smear the sleeping guards with blood.

Macbeth. I won't go again. I am afraid to think what I have done. I dare not look on it again.

Lady Macbeth. Weak of purpose! Give me the daggers. The sleeping and the dead are like pictures. Only a child fears a painted devil. If he is bleeding, I'll gild[6] the faces of the sleeping guards with his blood, for it must seem to be their guilt.

[Lady Macbeth *exits with the daggers. There is a loud knocking sound offstage. Someone is knocking on the large gate at the front of the castle. If Macbeth and Lady Macbeth are found now with blood on them, they will be executed.*]

Macbeth. What is that knocking? Why does every noise frighten me? [*He looks at his bloody hands.*] What hands are here! Ha, they pull out my eyes. Will all great Neptune's[7] oceans wash this blood off my hands? No, my hand will turn all the green seas red.

---

[6] gild—to put a nice finish, often gold, over something that isn't as nice. *Wordplay:* Lady Macbeth is making a pun (a type of joke where a word has different meanings). The pun is on "gilt," to gild an object, and "guilt," which means a person feels badly about something he or she shouldn't have done.

[7] Neptune's—referring to the god of the sea.

[*Enter* Lady Macbeth. *She now has blood on her hands.*]

Lady Macbeth. My hands are the same color, but I would be ashamed to have a heart so white.[8] [*There is more knocking.*] I hear knocking at the south gate. Let's go to our room. A little water washes off this deed. How easy it is, then! You are too upset. [*Another knock.*] Hark, more knocking. Get on your dressing gown, or we will be caught. Be not lost in such poor-spirited thoughts.

Macbeth. Knowing what I have done, it were best I didn't know myself. [*Another knock.*] Wake Duncan with your knocking. I wish you could.

[*They exit.*]

---

[8] white—often stands for cowardice.

ACT TWO, SCENE THREE

At the castle gate, the porter lets in Macduff. Macduff discovers the murdered king. Macbeth kills the king's body-guards and blames them for the murder. The king's two sons plan to leave the country for fear that they will be murdered next.[1]

[*More knocking. The* Porter, *who is drunk, enters.*]

Porter. Here's a lot of knocking indeed! If I were the porter at the gate of hell, I would have to turn the key plenty of times to let everyone in. [*More knocking.*] Knock, knock, knock! Who's there, in the name of Beelzebub?[2] Here's a farmer who hanged himself because he couldn't make a big profit by charging poor people too

---

[1] This scene is often called the "Porter Scene." It gave the audience a short break from the rest of the tragedy.

[2] Beelzebub—the chief devil in hell.

much for their food. Come in![3] You'll need a lot of handkerchiefs because you're going to sweat a lot here. Knock, knock! Who's there, in the other devil's name? I believe that here's an **equivocator**[4] that can swear opposite things are true, who lied about treason, yet could not lie to heaven. O, come in, equivocator. [*Another knock.*] Knock, knock, knock! Who's there? I believe here's an English tailor who makes French-looking clothes and steals a little cloth as he does it. Come in, tailor. Here you may roast your goose.[5] [*Another knock.*] Knock, knock! Never quiet. Who's out there? This place is too cold for hell. I won't be a porter at the gate of hell any longer. I thought I'd show all that go down the primrose path on the way to the everlasting bonfire.[6] [*Another knock.*] Right away, right away!

[*The* porter *opens the door and lets in* Macduff *and* Lennox.]

---

[3] The porter pretends to be the gate-keeper in hell, letting in people he doesn't like.

[4] **equivocator**—someone who deliberately confuses the listeners by picking words that have more than one meaning or saying one thing but thinking another.

[5] A tailor's goose is an iron.

[6] The porter is putting down people with better jobs than his. "The primrose path to the everlasting bonfire" is the pleasant way to hell.

Porter. I pray you, remember to give the porter a tip.

Macduff. Did you go to bed so late, friend, that you sleep so late this morning?

Porter. In truth, sir, we were partying until the second time the rooster crowed (at three in the morning). And drink causes three things.

Macduff. What three things does drink cause?

Porter. In truth, sir, it causes a red nose, sleep, and urine. Sex, sir, it starts and stops. It causes the desire, but it takes away the performance. Therefore, much drink is an equivocator with desire. It makes him and ruins him, makes him stand to and not stand to; finally, it equivocates him to sleep and, giving him the lie,[7] leaves him.

Macduff. I believe drink gave you the lie last night.

Porter. That it did, sir. It grabbed me by the throat and threw me down. But, I got back at drink for his lie. I was too strong for him, though he grabbed my legs. But I threw him out.

---

[7] lie—a wrestling term, meaning to throw someone down. *Wordplay:* Drink throws people down. This is a pun. *Lie* also means both to lie down and to tell an untruth.

Macduff. Is Macbeth awake yet?

[*Enter* Macbeth.]

Our knocking has wakened him. Here he comes.

[*The* Porter *exits.*]

Lennox. Good morning, noble sir.

Macbeth. Good morning to both of you.

Macduff. Is the king awake, worthy thane?

Macbeth. Not yet.

Macduff. He commanded me to meet him early this morning. I am almost late.

Macbeth. I'll take you to him.

Macduff. I know this is a joyful trouble to you, but it is a trouble.

Macbeth. The work we like to do cures pain. This is the door.

Macduff. I'll be so bold as to enter. It is my duty.

[Macduff *enters the king's rooms.*]

Lennox. Does the king leave today?

Macbeth. He does. He planned to.

Lennox. This was a wild night.[8] Where we were, heavy winds and strange cries were heard, screams of death, and predictions of terrible things to come, much confusion. The owl screamed all night. Some say there were earthquakes.

Macbeth. It was a rough night.[9]

Lennox. My young memory cannot remember a worse one.

[*Enter* Macduff.]

Macduff. O horror, horror, horror! Tongue nor heart can neither conceive nor name thee![10]

Macbeth and Lennox. What's the matter?

Macduff. Destruction has made his masterpiece. Most unholy murder has broken open the head chosen by God and stolen its life.

Macbeth. What is it you say? The life?

Lennox. Do you mean the king?

---

[8] In early times, people often believed that when something bad happened to a great man, nature acted in strange ways.

[9] This is an understatement. This wasn't just a "rough night" for Macbeth. It was probably the worst night of his life.

[10] Tongue nor heart can neither conceive nor name thee—neither can we speak or feel such horror.

Macduff. Approach the room and ruin your sight with a new Gorgon.[11] Do not ask me to speak. See and then speak yourselves.

[Macbeth *and* Lennox *enter the king's rooms.*]

Macduff. Awake! Awake! Ring the alarm bell. Murder and treason! Banquo and Donalbain, Malcolm, awake! Shake off sleep, which looks like death, and look on death itself. Up, up, and see the picture of the end of us all. Malcolm, Banquo, as from your graves rise up and walk like ghosts to see this horror. Ring the alarm bell.

[*There is much noise. The alarm bell rings.* Soldiers *run out. People are dressed for sleeping. No one knows what's happening.*]

[*Enter* Lady Macbeth.]

Lady Macbeth. What is wrong that such a hideous trumpet calls us from our sleep to meet? Speak, speak!

Macduff. [*To* Lady Macbeth] O gentle lady, it is not for you to hear what I can speak. Repeating it in a woman's ear would kill her as she heard it.[12]

---

[11] Gorgon—horror. In mythology, when a person looked on one of the three women called Gorgons, that person would turn to stone.

[12] This is *dramatic irony*. Hearing about the king's death wouldn't kill Lady Macbeth because she helped plan it.

[*Enter* Banquo.]

O Banquo, Banquo, the king is murdered.

Lady Macbeth. Woe, alas! What, in our house?

Banquo. It is too cruel anywhere. Dear Duff,[13] I beg you, say this isn't so.

[*Enter* Macbeth, Lennox, *and* Ross.]

Macbeth. If I had died an hour before this happened, I would have lived long enough. From this time on there's nothing important in life. Everything is just a toy. Fame and honor is dead. The good wine of life has been used up, and the bitter wine is all that is left.

[*Enter* Malcolm *and* Donalbain.]

Donalbain. What is wrong?

Macbeth. You are, and do not know it. The spring, the head, the source of your blood is stopped; the very source of it is stopped.

Macduff. Your royal father's murdered.

Malcolm. Oh! Who did this?

Lennox. The men who guarded him, it seems, had done it. Their hands and faces were all covered with blood. So were their daggers, which we

---

[13] Duff—a nickname for Macduff.

found unwiped beside them. They stared and were confused. No man could trust them.

Macbeth. O, yet I am sorry I was so angry that I killed them.

Macduff. Why did you do that?[14]

Macbeth. Who can be wise, amazed, calm and angry, loyal and fair, in one moment? No man. My strong love for the king caused me not to pause and think. Here lay Duncan, his silver skin covered with his golden blood. His stabs looked like unnatural breaks in the wall of a fort for death's entrance. There lay the murderers, covered in the red of their trade, their daggers improperly covered with blood and flesh instead of properly put away. Who could keep from acting that loved the king and had the courage to do something for that love?

[Macbeth *has said and done too much. Possibly,* Lady Macbeth *fakes fainting to draw attention away from him. Or she is shocked that he would lose control.*]

Lady Macbeth. Help me, oh!

Macduff. Help the lady.

---

[14] Macduff wants to know why Macbeth killed the suspected guards. Now they have no one to question. The guards had nothing to gain by killing the king, so if they did it, someone else paid them.

Malcolm. [*Aside to* Donalbain] We should say something. Some may claim that we did this.

Donalbain. [*Aside to* Malcolm] What should we say? We don't know who did it. They may catch us unprepared and rush on us. Let's leave. This happened so fast our tears haven't yet come.

Malcolm. [*Aside to* Donalbain] We have not begun to feel our strong sorrow.

Banquo. Help the lady.

[Lady Macbeth *is carried out.*]

Banquo. When we have dressed, let us meet and ask questions about this most bloody work. Fears and suspicions shake us. I trust in God that we will find the hidden reason for this murder. I fight against this evil treason.

Macduff. And so do I.

All. [*There should be different wordings from the crowd, but they should say something like "Yes" and "So do I."*]

Macbeth. Let us dress for action and meet in the hall.

All. [*Once again there should be different answers, but they should show that the crowd wishes to follow Macbeth's orders.*]

[*All but* Malcolm *and* Donalbain *exit.*]

Malcolm. What will you do? Let's not stay with them. It's easy for a traitor to act as if he is sad. I'll go to England and ask the English king for help.

Donalbain. And I'll go to Ireland. It will be safer if we are not in the same place. Where we are, there's daggers in men's smiles.[15] The closer we are related in blood to Duncan, the closer we are to being bloody.

Malcolm. This murdering is not over yet. Our safest way is to leave. Therefore, to our horses. Let's not be too polite in saying good-bye. There's a reason to steal away when we are stealing our lives from a place without mercy.

[*They exit.*]

---

[15] there's daggers in men's smiles—smiling men may kill us with their daggers.

Outside the castle, Ross and an old man talk about the strange things that happened on the night the king was murdered. Macduff says that the king's two sons have been blamed for hiring the murderers and that Macbeth has been named king.

[*Enter* Ross *with an* Old Man.]

Old Man. Seventy years I can remember well. In that time I have seen dreadful times and strange things, but this terrible night makes all others look like nothing.

Ross. Ha, good father, even the threatening heavens are troubled with man's acts. By the clock it is day, and yet night covers the sun. Is it night's strength or day's shame that darkness covers the earth like a tomb when living light should kiss it?

Old Man. It's unnatural. Even like the deed that's done. Last Tuesday I saw a falcon killed by a small owl.[1]

Ross. And Duncan's horses (a thing most strange and true), beautiful and fast, the best horses, turned wild and broke out of their stalls. They wouldn't follow directions, as if they were at war with man.

Old Man. It is said that his horses bit each other.

Ross. They did. I was amazed when I saw it.

[*Enter* Macduff.]

Ross. Here comes the good Macduff. [*To* Macduff] How are things going now, sir?

Macduff. Why, can't you see?[2]

Ross. Is it known who did this more than bloody deed?

Macduff. The guards that Macbeth has killed.

Ross. Alas the day, what good did it do them?

---

[1] The old man saw the larger bird being killed by the smaller bird as a sign that the king was going to be killed by someone who wasn't as powerful or important.

[2] Macduff is afraid to say that things are going well or badly. Ross might be one of the murderers and might decide to kill Macduff if he says the wrong thing.

Macduff. They were secretly bribed. Malcolm and Donalbain, the King's two sons, have run away, which makes them look guilty.

Ross. That's unnatural! It is an unprofitable ambition that will eat up what gave it life. Then Macbeth will probably be named king.

Macduff. He has already been named king and gone to Scone[3] to be crowned.

Ross. Where is Duncan's body?

Macduff. Carried to Colmekill where his family is always buried.

Ross. Will you go to Scone to see Macbeth crowned?

Macduff. No, cousin, I'll go to my home in Fife.

Ross. Well, I'll go to Scone.

Macduff. Well, may you see things well done there. Good-bye, unless our old robes fit better than our new.[4] Good-bye.

Ross. [*to the* Old Man] Farewell, father.[5]

---

[3] Scone—Scottish kings were crowned outside at Scone. The new king stood on a large stone, called the Stone of Scone, which today is under the throne of Great Britain in London. All the leaders would go to show their loyalty to the new king.

[4] our old robes fit better than our new—our old king may be better than our new king.

[5] father—Ross is using a title of respect. The old man is not actually his father.

Old Man. God's blessing go with you and with those that would make good out of bad and friends out of **foes.**[6]

[*They all exit.*]

---

[6] **foes**—enemies. The old man's words seem to be a good paradox.

In the king's palace at Forres, Banquo says he suspects Macbeth of murdering Duncan. Banquo hopes the witches' prediction for his family comes true. Macbeth invites Banquo to a banquet. Macbeth hires two murderers to kill Banquo and Fleance.

[*Enter* Banquo.]

Banquo. [*Aside*] You have it now—king, Cawdor, Glamis, all, as the weird women promised, and I fear you deeply sinned to get it. Yet, the same women said that your family would not keep the kingship, but I would father many kings. If these women tell any truth, and they have told you truth, why, by the truths they told you, may they not be my fortune tellers as well and set me up in hope? But hush, no more.

[*The trumpets sound to announce the entrance of* Macbeth, *who is now king. With him are* Lady Macbeth, Lennox, Ross, Lords, *and* Attendants.]

Macbeth. [*Pointing to* Banquo] Here's our chief guest.

Lady Macbeth. If he had been forgotten, there would be a gap in our great feast and everything would not be right.

Macbeth. Tonight we hold a formal banquet, sir, and I'll ask you to be there.

Banquo. Let your highness command me. My duties are forever tied to you.

Macbeth. Are you riding somewhere this afternoon?

Banquo. Yes, my good lord.

Macbeth. We[1] would have asked you to give us your good advice in today's meetings, but we'll ask for it tomorrow. Are you riding very far?

Banquo. As far as I can ride between now and supper. If my horse doesn't go as quickly as I think, I may be riding in the dark for an hour or two.

---

[1] Now that he is king, instead of saying "I," Macbeth uses the royal "we."

Macbeth. Do not fail to come to our feast.

Banquo. My lord, I will not.

Macbeth. We hear our bloody cousins, Malcolm and Donalbain, are in England and Ireland. They have not confessed to killing their father and are making up strange stories to explain the murders. But we will talk about that tomorrow when state business will bring us together. Get to your horse. Adieu,[2] until you return tonight. Does Fleance go with you?

Banquo. Yes, my good lord. It is getting late.

Macbeth. I wish your horses fast and sure of foot. So I send you to them. Farewell.

[Banquo *exits.*]

Let every man be master of his own time until seven this night. To enjoy your company all the more later, we will stay alone until suppertime. Until then, God be with you.

[*Everyone exits except* Macbeth *and his* Servant.]

Macbeth. Sirrah,[3] a word with you. Are those men I sent for waiting?

---

[2] Adieu—a French word meaning "good-bye."

[3] Sirrah—used to speak to someone below the speaker's social level.

Servant. They are waiting outside the castle gate, my lord.

Macbeth. Bring them before us.

[*The* Servant *exits.*]

Macbeth. [*To himself*] To be king is nothing. I must be king safely. I have a deep fear of Banquo. He is a noble leader. He dares to do much. Not only is he brave but he is wise enough to be careful. I fear no one but him. He scolded the Weird Sisters when they called me king and told them to speak to him. They predicted he would be the father to a line of kings. Upon my head they put a fruitless crown,[4] and put a barren scepter[5] in my hand. No son of mine will be king after me. If this is true, then I have dishonored myself for Banquo's children. For them I murdered the good King Duncan, ruined my peace, and gave away my soul to the devil. I have done all of this for the children of Banquo, to make them kings. Rather than that, come fate, let's battle to the death. [*To people entering stage*] Who's there?

[*Enter the* Servant *with two* Murderers *that* Macbeth *has invited.*]

---

[4] fruitless crown—a crown that he cannot pass on.

[5] barren scepter—"barren" means not capable of having children. A scepter is the rod the king carries as a symbol of his physical power. Macbeth will not be able to pass it on.

Macbeth. [*To the* Servant] Go, guard the door. Stay there until we call you.

[*The* Servant *exits.*]

Macbeth. Didn't we last speak yesterday?

Murderers. [*They speak slightly different words but say something like…*] It was, so please your highness.

Macbeth. Well then, have you thought about what I said? Now you've learned that in the past Banquo ruined your lives. I made this clear to you when last we talked, proved it to you. I showed you how he tricked you and shut you out, how he did it and who helped him— everything that was needed to prove to even a half-wit or crazy man that Banquo destroyed your lives.

First Murderer. You showed us.

Macbeth. I did so, and went further, and that is the point of our second meeting. Is your patience so strong that you can let this go on? Are you so religious that you pray for this man and his children when his heavy hand has ruined you for life and made your children poor?

First Murderer. We are men, my lord.

Macbeth. Yes, you are men. But hounds, grey-hounds, mongrels, spaniels, curs, lap dogs, water spaniels, and half wolves are all called dogs. We could list each dog and show its value: the slow, the clever, the watch dog, the hunter. Every one could be listed by the gift nature has given it. And men can be so listed. If you are at the top of the list and not at the bottom, say it, and I will give you something to do that will rid you of your enemy and make me reward you. We are not healthy as long as he lives. With his death we are perfect.

Second Murderer. My lord, the hits and blows of the world have made me so angry that I don't care what I do to punish the world.

First Murderer. And I am another, so weary with disasters and bad luck that I would gamble my life on any chance, either to fix my life or end it.

Macbeth. Both of you know Banquo was your enemy.

Murderers. True, my lord.

Macbeth. He is mine also. And so close that every minute he is alive is a stab at my heart. I could with pure power sweep him from my sight just because I want to, yet I must not, for some of my friends are his friends. When he dies, I must cry for him even though I struck him down.

That is why I need your help. You must hide this from the common eye for many serious reasons.

Second Murderer. We shall, my lord, do what you tell us to do.

First Murderer. Though our lives—[6]

Macbeth. Your courage shines through you. Within this hour I will tell you where to go and when to do it, for it must be done tonight and away from the castle. I must be kept clear of this. And with Banquo (to leave no mistakes in the work), Fleance, his son, who is with him, whose death is just as important to me, must meet the fate of that dark hour. Make up your minds. I'll hear you soon.

Murderers. We have made up our minds.

Macbeth. I'll be with you right away. Wait for me out there. [Macbeth *points offstage.*]

[*The* Murderers *exit.*]

Macbeth. It is concluded. Banquo, your soul's flight, if it finds heaven, must find it out tonight.

[Macbeth *exits.*]

---

[6] Macbeth interrupts the murderer because he does not care what the murderer is going to say. The murderers have said they will do what he wants. That's enough.

In the palace at Forres, Macbeth and Lady Macbeth discuss their unhappiness. Macbeth is planning to murder Banquo and Fleance without telling Lady Macbeth.

[*Enter* Lady Macbeth *and a* Servant.]

Lady Macbeth. Is Banquo gone from the court?

Servant. Yes, madam, but he returns tonight.

Lady Macbeth. Tell the king that if he has time, I would like to speak with him.

Servant. Madam, I will.

[*The* Servant *exits.*]

Lady Macbeth. We have nothing and have spent everything when we get what we want but are not happy. It's safer to be that which we destroy than by destruction live in doubtful joy.

[*Enter* Macbeth, *who looks unhappy.*]

How are you, my lord? Why do you stay alone imagining sad things, paying attention to thoughts that should have died with the people you think about? Things without all remedy should be without regard.[1] What's done is done.

Macbeth. We have slashed the snake that threatens us, but not killed it. It will heal, and we'll be in danger again. But, let everything fall apart, both heaven and earth suffer, before we will eat our meal in fear, and sleep with these terrible dreams that shake us every night. Better to be with the dead, whom we, to gain our peace, have sent to peace, than to lie awake tortured by our own mind in wild sleeplessness. Duncan is in his grave. After this fitful fever of life, he sleeps well. **Treason**[2] has done its worst. Swords or poison, traitors at home, foreign armies— nothing can touch Duncan anymore.

Lady Macbeth. Come on, my noble lord, smooth over your worried face. Be bright and happy with our guests tonight.

---

[1] Things without all remedy should be without regard—What we can't fix, we shouldn't think about.

[2] **Treason**—attempt to overthrow the legal government.

Macbeth. I will, my love, and so I pray be you. Pay special attention to Banquo. Give him special honor with your words and looks even while we plan for him to be unsafe. We must keep our reputations by flattering and make our faces into masks that hide what is in our hearts, disguising what we really are.

Lady Macbeth. You must stop this.

Macbeth. O, full of **scorpions**[3] is my mind, dear wife! You know that Banquo and his son Fleance are still alive.

Lady Macbeth. But they will not live forever.

Macbeth. That's a comfort. They can be hurt. Then be happy. Before the bat flies his lonely flight, before Hecate calls the beetle in humming flight to announce night's yawning start, there shall be done a dreadful deed.

Lady Macbeth. What's to be done?

Macbeth. Be innocent of the knowledge, dearest one, until you **applaud**[4] the deed. [Macbeth *turns away as if in prayer*.]

---

[3] **scorpions**—insects with a poisonous stinger at the tip of a long tail.
[4] **applaud**—praise.

Come, blinding night,
Scarf[5] up the tender eye of pitiful day,
And with thy bloody and invisible hand
Cancel and tear to pieces that great bond
Which keeps me pale! Light thickens, and the crow
Makes wing to the rooky[6] wood.
Good things of day begin to droop and drowse,[7]
Whiles night's black agents to their **preys**[8] do rouse.[9]

[*To* Lady Macbeth] You are surprised at my words, but listen. Things started with evil make themselves strong by doing more evil. So, I beg you, go with me.

[*They exit.*]

---

[5] scarf—cover, as with a scarf.

[6] rooky—full of rooks, birds.

[7] drowse—get sleepy.

[8] **preys**—victims.

[9] These eight well-known lines are Shakespeare's own.

In a park near the palace, the two murderers are joined by another. They kill Banquo, but Fleance escapes.

[*Enter three* Murderers.]

First Murderer. But, who told you to join us?

Third Murderer. Macbeth.

Second Murderer. We shouldn't mistrust him since he tells us exactly what we have to do.

First Murderer. Then stay with us. The sun hasn't set yet. This is when the late traveler rushes to get home, and the people we are waiting for must almost be here.

Third Murderer. Hark, I hear horses.

Banquo. [*Offstage*] Give us a light there!

Second Murderer. It's him. The rest who are expected are already at the court.

First Murderer. His horses are going a different way.

Third Murderer. They take the horses almost a mile away, but from here to the inner gate men usually walk.

[*Enter* Banquo *and* Fleance, *carrying a torch.*]

Second Murderer. [*To the other* Murderers] A light, a light!

Third Murderer. [*To the other* Murderers] It's him.

First Murderer. [*To the other* Murderers] Get ready.

Banquo. [*To* Fleance] It will rain tonight.

First Murderer. Let it come down!¹

[*The three* Murderers *attack* Banquo *and* Fleance. *As in most scenes of action, many of the words will be shouted and blurred together. The actors would add words to the script, but Shakespeare has written lines to guide the actors.*]

---

¹ Let it come down—*Wordplay:* This is a murderer's joke. Let the rain come down; let the knives come down.

Banquo. O treachery! Run, good Fleance, run, run, run! Live to **avenge**[2] me—O **villain**![3]

[Banquo *is killed.* Fleance *escapes and exits.*][4]

Third Murderer. Who knocked out the light?

First Murderer. Wasn't that what we were supposed to do?

Third Murderer. There's but one dead. The son has run away.

Second Murderer. We have lost half of what we were supposed to do.

First Murderer. Well, let's get away and say how much was done.

[*The* Murderers *exit.*]

---

[2] **avenge**—get back at the people who hurt you. Punish.

[3] **villain**—evil person.

[4] This was a fight scene. It's not very exciting to read, but the actors would make it a very exciting scene to watch. When reading a play, you have to picture what might happen because the stage directions give only the smallest idea.

At a banquet in the palace, one of the murderers reports that Banquo is dead. The ghost of Banquo appears to Macbeth. Lady Macbeth sends the guests away. Macbeth decides to visit the witches to learn what else may happen.

[*A banquet.*[1] *Enter* Macbeth, Lady Macbeth, Ross, Lennox, Lords, *and* Attendants.]

Macbeth. You know where your rank entitles you to sit; sit down. A hearty welcome to everyone.

[*Everyone sits.*]

Lords. [*The actors would say different things, but in general…*] Thanks to your Majesty.

Macbeth. Ourself will walk and sit with you and play the humble host. Our hostess, Lady

---

[1] This is the banquet that Macbeth told Banquo not to miss.

Macbeth, will stay here at the head table, but we will ask her to welcome you.

Lady Macbeth. Say it for me, sir, to all our friends, for my heart says they are welcome.

[*The first* Murderer *enters, off to the side.*]

Macbeth. See, my wife, our guests return your welcome with their hearts' thanks. Both sides are even.[2] I'll sit in the middle of you all. Hold nothing back: enjoy yourselves. Soon I'll give the toast. [Macbeth *goes to the* Murderer *and speaks to him in a low voice.*] There's blood on your face.

First Murderer. It's Banquo's blood then.

Macbeth. Banquo's blood looks better on the outside of you than on the inside of him. Is he killed?

First Murderer. My lord, his throat is cut. That I did for him.

Macbeth. You are the best of cut-throats, yet he's good that did the same thing to Fleance. If you did it, you are without equal.

---

[2] *Wordplay:* The thanks of the guests equal the welcome of Lady Macbeth, and there are equal numbers on both sides of the table.

First Murderer. Most royal sir, Fleance escaped.

Macbeth. [*To himself*] Then comes my anger and fear again. I would have felt safe, as solid as a rock, as free as the wind, but now I am closed in, cramped, bound by doubts and fears. [*To the* Murderer] But Banquo's safe?[3]

First Murderer. Yes, my lord. He's safe in a ditch, with twenty deep cuts on his head, the smallest of which would have killed him.

Macbeth. Thanks for that. There the grown serpent lies.[4] The worm that has run away will be poisonous in the future, but he has no teeth now. Now go. Tomorrow I'll talk to you again.

[*The* Murderer *exits.*]

Lady Macbeth. My royal lord, you do not welcome your guests. They might as well be eating at an inn or at home if they do not have your good will and attention.

[Banquo's Ghost *enters and sits where* Macbeth *planned to sit.* Macbeth *at first does not see the ghost.*][5]

---

[3] Banquo's safe?—Macbeth is asking if Banquo is safely dead.

[4] Macbeth calls Banquo a serpent, a poisonous snake. He next calls Fleance a worm, a young snake. He cannot hurt Macbeth now, but could in the future.

[5] The director must decide how the ghost will be shown. The ghost doesn't talk. In Shakespeare's time, the ghost was shown on stage as a gray and murdered Banquo, but only Macbeth could see it. Today, the ghost is sometimes not shown or is only hinted at, perhaps with a light where it should be.

Macbeth. [*He raises his wine glass to give the toast.*] Now, good eating and good appetite, and health come after both!

Lennox. May it please your highness to sit here. [Lennox *points to the empty chair.*]

Macbeth. Here we would have all the great men of our country under one roof if Banquo were only with us. I hope I can blame him for unkindly staying away and not pity him for having some accident.

Ross. His absence, sir, looks bad because he did promise to be here. Please, your highness, honor us with your royal company.

Macbeth. The table is full.

Lennox. Here is a place we saved for you, sir.

Macbeth. Where?

Lennox. Here, my good lord. [Macbeth *sees the ghost and shows his surprise and fear.*] What has upset your highness?

Macbeth. Which of you has done this?

Lords. [*Each person will say something slightly different, but in general...*] What, my good lord?

Macbeth. [*To the* Ghost] You cannot say I did it. Don't shake your bloody head at me.

Ross. Gentlemen, rise. His highness is not well.

Lady Macbeth. Sit, worthy friends. The king has often had these fits since his youth. Pray you, stay here. The fit will only last a moment. In a second he will be well again. If you notice him too much, you will upset him more and make it worse. Eat and pay no attention. [*She pulls* Macbeth *to the side and says to him*] Are you a man?

Macbeth. Yes, and a bold one, that dares to look on that which would horrify the devil.

Lady Macbeth. O, false stuff! This is a picture drawn by your fear. This is like the dagger in the air that you said led you to Duncan. O, these outbursts, these false fears would sound good in women's stories told by the fire in winter by an old grandmother. For shame! Why do you make such faces? When all's done, you are just looking at an empty stool.[6]

---

[6] Macbeth sees a ghost, not an empty place at the table.

Macbeth. I pray you, see there. Behold, look! [*To the ghost*] What do you want, what do you say? What do I care? If you can nod your head, speak too. If tombs and graves send back those that we bury, we should let the birds of prey[7] eat the dead.

[*The* Ghost *disappears.*]

Lady Macbeth. Your foolishness has destroyed your manhood.

Macbeth. As I stand here, I say I saw him.

Lady Macbeth. Fie, for shame!

Macbeth. Blood has been shed in the old times before human law made life gentle. Yes, and more recently too, there have been murders too terrible to hear about. The time has been that when the brains were out, the man would die, and that would be the end. But now they rise again with twenty deadly wounds on their heads and push us off our stools. This is more strange than such a murder is.

Lady Macbeth. My worthy lord, your noble friends want you to rejoin them.

---

[7] birds of prey—birds that eat meat, like hawks, vultures, and ravens.

Macbeth. I do forget. Do not wonder at this, my most worthy friends. I have a strange illness, which is nothing to those that know me. Come, love and health to all. Then I'll sit down. Give me some wine. Fill the cups full.

[*The* Ghost *appears.*]

Macbeth. I drink to the general joy of the whole table and to our dear friend Banquo, whom we miss. I wish he were here! To all of you and to him, we drink. Let us all drink to all of us.

Lords. [*There are many different responses, but in general...*] Our duties, and our promises.

[*They all raise their glasses, but* Macbeth *sees the* Ghost *and throws his full cup at it, screaming.*]

Macbeth. [*To the* Ghost] Be gone, quit my sight! Let the earth hide you. You're not real. Your blood is cold. Those eyes that glare at me can't see.

Lady Macbeth. Think of this, good lords, as something that often happens and causes no real trouble. That's all it is; only, it spoils the pleasure of our party.

Macbeth. [*To the* Ghost] What any man dares to do, I dare to do. Approach me looking like a rugged Russian bear, a rhinoceros, or a tiger. Take any shape but the one you have now, and my firm nerves shall never tremble. Or be alive again and dare me to fight you with swords in a deserted place. If I tremble in fear and won't fight, call me a baby girl. Get away, horrible shadow! Unreal thing that mocks me, be gone! [*The* Ghost *disappears.*] Why so, when it is gone, I am a man again. [Macbeth *realizes everyone is staring at him, so he speaks to the crowd.*] I beg you to sit still.

Lady Macbeth. You have ruined the joy, broken up this good party with amazing confusion.

Macbeth. Can such things be and overcome us like a sudden summer storm without our wondering what is happening? I have seen and done horrible things but I am amazed that you can look on such sights and keep the color in your cheeks when mine are white with fear.

Ross. What sights, my lord?

Lady Macbeth. I pray you, speak not. He grows worse and worse. Questions anger him. Good night to all of you. Don't be formal in going, but go at once.

Lennox. Good night, and better health come to his majesty.

Lady Macbeth. A kind good night to all.

[*Exit all except* Macbeth *and* Lady Macbeth.]

Macbeth. It will have blood, they say; blood will have blood. Stones have been known to move, and trees to speak; magic and prophecy have used strange ways to show a secret murderer. What time is it?

Lady Macbeth. The end of night or early morning. I cannot tell which.

Macbeth. What do you say about Macduff's not coming to see us though I asked him.

Lady Macbeth. Did you send for him, sir?

Macbeth. I will send for him. I hear about him. I pay a servant in everyone's home to spy for me. Tomorrow (and quickly) I will go to the Weird Sisters. They will tell me more, for now I wish more than anything to know by the worst means the worst things. For my own good, all others shall fall. I have waded into a stream of blood so far that I might as well wade the rest of the way rather than turn back. I am thinking of doing things I would never have done before. Things that I must do. I must act out these things before they can be thought about.

Lady Macbeth. You are not getting what all nature needs, sleep.

Macbeth. Come, we'll go to sleep. My strange fears are the fears of a beginner who hasn't had enough practice. We are but young in actions.

[*They exit.*]

ACT THREE, SCENE FIVE

On the heath, Hecate, the goddess of the evil part of the
night and protector of witches, scolds the witches for med-
dling and makes her own plans to destroy Macbeth.

[*Thunder. Enter the three* Witches. *They meet* Hecate,
the goddess of witchcraft.]

First Witch. Why, how are you, Hecate? You
look angry.

Hecate. Don't I have a right to be angry, ugly old
women that you are? You push me too much
and don't respect me enough. How did you
dare to play with Macbeth in riddles and death
when I, the real power and planner of all harm,
was never called to play my part or show the
glory of our evil art? And what is worse, all that
you have done is only for a bad son, an angry
boy, who loves to do evil, as others do, for his

own gains, not for ours. You must make up for this now. Get you gone. And meet me in the morning at the pit of hell. There he will come to see his future. Bring what you need to cast our magical spells. I will fly through the air now. This night I will do things that will cause sorrow and death. I have great business to do before noon. On the corner of the moon hangs a poisonous drop. I'll catch it before it falls. And that drop, fixed with my magic tricks, will make false spirits which will cause Macbeth to destroy himself. He shall think that he can overcome fate and not be killed. He will place his hopes higher than wisdom, virtue, and fear. And, you all know, overconfidence is mortals'[1] chief enemy.

[*Music and a song.*]

Hecate. Hark! I am called. My little spirit, see, sits in a foggy cloud and waits for me.

[Hecate *exits. There is more singing, "Come away, come away."*]

First Witch. Come, let's be quick. She'll be back soon.

[*They exit.*]

---

[1] mortals'—belonging to humans who will die, unlike gods and witches.

*In the palace at Forres, Lennox and another lord discuss
what they know: Macbeth is the murderer; the murdered
king's oldest son, Malcolm, is safe in England; and Macduff
has gone there to seek help against Macbeth.*

[*Enter* Lennox *and a* Lord.]

Lennox. I agree with what you were saying, and
we can make more good guesses. Things have
been done strangely. The gracious Duncan was
pitied by Macbeth; he is dead. And brave
Banquo walked too late at night, who you may
say Fleance killed, for Fleance ran away. Men
must not walk too late at night. We all know it
was horrible for Malcolm and Donalbain to kill
their good father.[1] Damned crime. How it

---

[1] Lennox and the lord know that Macbeth is guilty, but they have to be
careful what they say. Macbeth has spies everywhere. They use *irony*, saying
one thing, but meaning the opposite.

grieved Macbeth! Didn't he kill the two drunken guards in anger? Wasn't that a noble action? Yes, and wise, too, because it would have made anyone angry to hear them deny they had killed the king. So I say Macbeth has done everything well. And, I think if he had Duncan's sons locked up (and I hope he never shall) they would find out what happens when someone kills a father. So should Fleance. But peace. For speaking honestly and because he failed to come to Macbeth, I hear Macduff is in disgrace. Sir, do you know where he is?

Lord. Malcolm, the son of Duncan, from whom this tyrant Macbeth stole the throne, lives in England. He is under the protection of the pious English king, Edward. Macduff has gone there to ask the holy king for help, and to ask Northumberland and the warlike general Siward of Northumberland for help (with the aid of God). With their help, we may give meat to our tables, sleep to our nights, free our feasts from bloody knives, be true to our true king, and receive freely given honors—all of these things that we long for now. And this report has so upset Macbeth that he prepares for war.

Lennox. Did Macbeth send for Macduff?

Lord. He did. And Macduff answered, "Sir, not I." Macbeth's messenger seemed to say, "You'll be sorry you didn't obey."

Lennox. That should be a warning to Macduff to be careful and stay as far away from Macbeth as possible. We must pray that some holy angel flies to the court of England and tells of our problems even before Macduff arrives, so that a swift blessing may save our suffering country from the cursed hand of Macbeth.

Lord. I'll send my prayers with Macduff.

[*They exit.*]

In a cave, a large boiling pot bubbles. The witches show Macbeth three false spirits who give three new predictions: to beware of Macduff; that he cannot be beaten in battle until Birnam Wood moves to Dunsinane Hill; and that he cannot be killed by any man born of woman. Macbeth learns that Banquo's descendants will one day rule. Learning that Macduff has gone to England, Macbeth plans to kill Macduff's wife and children.

[*Enter the three* Witches.]

First Witch. Three times the striped cat has mewed.

Second Witch. Three times and one the hedgehog whined.

Third Witch. A demon cries "It's time, it's time!"

First Witch. Round about the cauldron[1] go;
In the poisoned entrails[2] throw.

---

[1] cauldron—witch's cooking pot.

[2] entrails—intestines or guts.

First, boil in the charmed pot,
A toad that poisonous sleep has got.

[*The* Witches *dance around the cauldron.*][3]

All. Double, double toil and trouble;
    Fire burn, and cauldron bubble.

Second Witch. Fillet of a fenny snake,
    In the cauldron boil and bake;
    Eye of newt, and toe of frog,
    Wool of bat, and tongue of dog,
    Adder's fork, and blindworm's sting,
    Lizard's leg, and howlet's wing;
    For a charm of pow'rful trouble
    Like a hell-broth boil and bubble.

All. Double, double toil and trouble;
    Fire burn, and cauldron bubble.

Third Witch. Scale of dragon, tooth of wolf,
    Witch's mummy, maw and gulf
    Of the ravined salt-sea shark,
    Root of hemlock, digged i' the dark;
    Liver of blaspheming Jew,
    Gall of goat, and slips of yew

---

[3] The witches sing a spell as they brew their ghastly stew. It includes animal guts (entrails, chaudron), a slice of swamp snake, eye of a salamander (newt), snake's tongue (adder's fork), a lizard's leg (leg of a blindworm), baby owl's (howlet's) wing, shark's stomach and throat (maw and gulf), the finger of a baby strangled by a prostitute (drab), and other gruesome things. These next twenty-nine lines are in Shakespeare's original words.

Slivered in the moon's eclipse;
Nose of Turk and Tartar's lips;
Finger of birth-strangled babe
Ditch-delivered by a drab:
Make the gruel thick and slab.
Add thereto a tiger's chaudron
For the ingredients of our cauldron.

All. Double, double toil and trouble;
Fire burn, and cauldron bubble.

Second Witch. Cool it with a baboon's blood.
Then the charm is firm and good.

[*Enter* Hecate, *who speaks to the other* Witches.]

Hecate. O, well done! Thanks for your pains.
And everyone shall share the gains.
And now around the cauldron sing
Like elves and fairies in a ring,
Enchanting all that you put in.

[*Music and a song.* Hecate *exits.*]

Second Witch. By the pricking of my thumbs,
Something wicked this way comes.
Open locks,
Whoever knocks!

[*Enter* Macbeth.]

Macbeth. How now, you secret, black, and midnight hags? What is it you do?

All. A deed without a name.

Macbeth. I solemnly call on you by that which you believe, however you come to know it, answer me. Though you untie the winds and let them fight against the churches, though the foaming waves confuse and sink ships, though farmer's crops and trees be blown down, though castles fall on their guards' heads, though palaces and pyramids fall to their foundations, though the very seeds from which new things grow are destroyed, even till destruction sickens everything, answer the questions I ask.

First Witch. Speak.

Second Witch. Demand.

Third Witch. We'll answer.

First Witch. Say if you would rather hear it from our mouths or from our masters'.

Macbeth. Call them. Let me see them.

First Witch. Pour the blood of a sow that has eaten her nine piglets; throw into the flame grease sweated from a murderer's **gallows**.[4]

---

[4] **gallows**—a wooden frame on which criminals are executed by hanging.

All. Come high or low; yourselves and your message quickly show.

[*Thunder.* First Apparition,[5] *a head wearing a war helmet, rises from the cauldron.*]

Macbeth. Tell me, you unknown power—

First Witch. He knows your thoughts. Hear his speech but say nothing.

First Apparition. Macbeth! Macbeth! Macbeth! Beware Macduff! Beware the thane of Fife![6] Dismiss me. Enough.

[*The* Apparition *exits into the cauldron.*]

Macbeth. Whatever you are, for your good warning, thanks. You have hit on my fear. But one word more—

First Witch. He will not be commanded. Here's another more powerful than the first.

[*Thunder. The* Second Apparition *rises up. It is a bloody child.*]

Second Apparition. Macbeth! Macbeth! Macbeth!—

Macbeth. If I had three ears, I'd hear you.

---

[5] Apparition—a supernatural thing, a ghost, a strange appearance. Shakespeare's stage had trap doors, so the "apparitions" could come up through the trap doors and seemed to appear out of the cauldron. Hecate, the chief witch, has called up false spirits to trick Macbeth into being too confident, and this will lead to his destruction and death.

[6] thane of Fife—Macduff.

Second Apparition. Be bloody, brave, and **resolute.**[7] Laugh to scorn the power of any man for none of woman born shall harm Macbeth.

[Second Apparition *exits into the cauldron.*]

Macbeth. Then live, Macduff, live, why should I fear you? But yet I'll be double sure and make a contract with fate[8] for my safety. Macduff shall not live, so I may tell pale-hearted fear it lies, and sleep in spite of thunder.

[*Thunder.* Third Apparition, *a child wearing a crown, with a tree in his hand, rises from the cauldron.*]

Macbeth. What is this that rises like the child of a king and on his baby head wears a crown?

Witches. Listen, but speak not to it.

Third Apparition. Be lion-brave, proud, and do not care who is hurt, who worries, or where enemies are. Macbeth will never be beaten in battle until great Birnam Wood[9] shall come against him to high Dunsinane Hill.

[Third Apparition *exits into the cauldron.*]

Macbeth. That will never happen. Who can make the forest move, tell a tree to unfix its root and

---

[7] **resolute**—determined, firm.

[8] Macbeth will leave nothing to chance. He wants complete control.

[9] Birnam Wood—a forest near Dunsinane Hill where Macbeth's castle, Inverness, stands.

walk? Sweet predictions, good! There will be no rebellion until Birnam Wood moves, and Macbeth shall live his natural life's length. Yet, my heart throbs to know one more thing. Tell me, if your power can tell so much: shall Banquo's family ever rule in this kingdom?

All. Do not ask any more.

Macbeth. I will be satisfied. Keep me from knowing this, and an eternal curse fall on you! Let me know!

[*The cauldron sinks through the trap door and music plays.*]

First Witch. Show!

Second Witch. Show!

Third Witch. Show!

All. Show his eyes and sadden his heart. Come like shadows, so depart.

[*Eight kings appear, the last one holds a mirror in which even more kings can be seen. After the last king comes* Banquo, *pointing at them to show they are his.*]

Macbeth. You look too much like the ghost of Banquo. Down! Your crown burns my eyes. And you all wear crowns and look like Banquo. A third is like the ones before it. [*To the* Witches]

Filthy hags, why do you show me this? A fourth? Burst out of my head, eyes! What, will the line of Banquo's kingly descendants stretch out to the end of time? Another yet? A seventh? I'll see no more. And yet the eighth[10] appears, who bears a mirror which shows me many more, and some I see rule over three countries and two religions.[11] Horrible sight. Now I see this is all true, for the blood-covered Banquo smiles at me and points at them as his.

[*This final* Apparition *exits.*]

Macbeth. Is all this true?

First Witch. Yes, sir, it is true. But why are you amazed? Come sisters, we will cheer him up. I'll use magic to make music while you dance around so this great king may say we welcomed him today.

[*Music. The* Witches *dance and disappear.*]

Macbeth. Where are they? Gone? Let this terrible hour be cursed in the calendar! [Macbeth *calls to guards he left outside.*] Come in, you outside.

[*Enter* Lennox.]

Did you see the Weird Sisters?

---

[10] the eighth—James I who paid Shakespeare to write this play.

[11] Banquo's descendants eventually ruled England, Scotland, and Ireland, which had two forms of Christianity: Catholicism and Protestantism.

Lennox. No, my lord.

Macbeth. Didn't they come by you?

Lennox. No, indeed, my lord.

Macbeth. Infected be the air they ride on, and to hell go all those that trust them! I heard horses. Who came here?

Lennox. A few men who brought news that Macduff is fled to England.

Macbeth. Fled to England?

Lennox. Yes, my good lord.

Macbeth. [*To himself*] Time, you guessed what terrible thing I was going to do. If we are going to do something, we must take action quickly. I will take action. Even now I will crown my thoughts with acts: I will surprise and take Macduff's castle at Fife, kill his wife, his babies, and all other unfortunate souls who are related to him in any way.[12] No boasting like a fool; this deed I'll do before my words cool. [*To Lennox*] Where are these gentlemen who brought this news? Take me to them.

[*They exit.*]

---

[12] Macbeth has gone another step toward evil. He is now killing people who do not stand in his way: women and babies.

ACT FOUR, SCENE TWO

In Macduff's castle at Fife, Lady Macduff is angry with her husband for leaving her and their family behind when he went to England. A messenger tells Lady Macduff that she is in danger. Murderers arrive from Macbeth to kill Lady Macduff and her son.

[*Enter* Lady Macduff, *her young* Son, *and* Ross.]

Lady Macduff. What has my husband done that makes him fly[1] our country?

Ross. You must have patience, madam.

Lady Macduff. He didn't have patience. His flight was madness. He was not a **traitor**,[2] but now he looks like one.

Ross. You don't know if he flew because of wisdom or fear.

[1] fly—run away from, flee.

[2] **traitor**—a person who commits treason by betraying his country.

Lady Macduff. Wisdom? Was it wise to leave his wife, to leave his babies, everything he owns, in a place where he himself is afraid to stay? He does not love us. He is unnatural. For the poor wren, the smallest of birds, will fight against the killer owl to save her young ones in the nest. He is all fear and has no love for us. There is little wisdom where the running runs against reason.

Ross. My dearest coz,[3] I beg you control your anger. Your husband is noble, wise, a good judge, and knows the terrible things that are happening in Scotland now. I dare not say much more. These are cruel times. We are called traitors and don't know why. We fear what we only hear rumors about. We are afraid, but don't know what we are afraid of. It's like floating on a wild and violent sea and being tossed about without control. I must leave. I will be back soon. When things are at their worst, they will stop or else get better. [*To Lady Macduff's* Son] My pretty cousin, blessing upon you.

Lady Macduff. He has a father, and yet he's fatherless.

---

[3] coz—cousin.

Ross. I am a fool to stay longer. If I stay, I will disgrace myself by crying, and you will be upset. I say good-bye at once.

[Ross *exits.*]

Lady Macduff. Sirrah, your father's dead.[4] What will you do now? How will you live?

Son. As birds live, Mother.

Lady Macduff. Will you eat worms and flies?

Son. I'll eat what I get. I mean, that's how birds live.

Lady Macduff. Poor bird, won't you be afraid of the traps set for birds?

Son. Why should I, mother? People don't hunt for poor birds. Besides, my father isn't dead, even though you say he is.

Lady Macduff. Yes, he is dead. What will you do for a father?

Son. No, what will you do for a husband?

Lady Macduff. I can buy twenty new husbands at any market.

---

[4] Lady Macduff is very upset with Macduff for leaving her and their children where Macbeth can get to them. Macduff's tragic flaw or defect is that he underestimates how evil Macbeth really is. He doesn't believe Macbeth will hurt innocent women and children.

Son. If you buy them, they won't make you happy, and you'll just sell them again.

Lady Macduff. You use up all your wisdom, yet it is wisdom enough for a child.

Son. Was my father a traitor, Mother?

Lady Macduff. Yes, he was.

Son. What is a traitor?

Lady Macduff. One who swears and lies.

Son. And is everyone a traitor who does that?

Lady Macduff. Everyone who does so is a traitor and must be hanged.

Son. And must they all be hanged that swear and lie?

Lady Macduff. Every one.

Son. Who must hang them?

Lady Macduff. Why, the honest men.

Son. Then the liars and swearers are fools, because there are more liars and swearers than honest men. There are enough liars and swearers to beat the honest men and hang them.[5]

---

[5] Lady Macduff means a traitor is one who swears an oath to be loyal to a king and lies about that oath, breaking the promise to the king. Her son thinks a traitor is one who swears (uses profanity/curses) and tells lies in general.

Lady Macduff. Now God help you, poor monkey! But what will you do for a father?

Son. If my father were dead, you'd cry for him. If you didn't cry, it would be a good sign that I should soon have a new father.

Lady Macduff. Poor talker, how you run on.

[*Enter a* Messenger, *out of breath, afraid.*]

Messenger. Bless you, fair lady. You don't know me, though I know how good you are. I know that you are in danger. If you will take a lowly man's advice, get out of here now. Go with your little ones! I am sorry to frighten you this way, but it would be cruelty not to warn you, and cruelty is coming near you now. Heaven help you! I dare not stay here any longer.

[*The* Messenger *exits.*]

Lady Macduff. Where should I fly? I have done no harm. But I remember now that I am in this world where to do harm is sometimes thought good, to do good is sometimes thought dangerous stupidity. Why then, alas, do I try to defend myself like a woman by saying that I have not hurt anyone?

[*Enter* Murderers.]

Who are these people?

Murderer. Where is your husband?

Lady Macduff. I hope he is not in a place so unholy that they would let someone like you find him.

Murderer. He's a traitor.

Son. You're a liar, you ugly villain!

Murderer. What do you say, baby? Child of a traitor!

[*The* Murderers *stab the* Son *repeatedly.*]

Son. He has killed me, Mother. Run away, I pray you.

Lady Macduff. [*She exits screaming*] Murder!

[Lady Macduff *is chased by the* Murderers, *who carry her* Son's *body offstage with them.*]

At the king's palace in England, Macduff begs Malcolm to return to Scotland and attack Macbeth. Malcolm tests Macduff and finds he is sincere. Ross tells Macduff of his family's murder. Macduff swears to get revenge.

[*Enter* Malcolm.]

Malcolm. Let us look for some sad shade and there weep until we can cry no more.

Macduff. Let us instead grab deadly swords and like good men fight to win back our fallen country. Every morning new widows howl, new orphans cry, new sorrows strike heaven on the face. Heaven cries with Scotland.

Malcolm. What I believe, I'll cry about; what I know, I'll believe; and what I can do, as I find the time, I will do. What you have said may perhaps be true. This tyrant, whose name alone blisters my tongue, was once thought honest. You have thought highly of him. He has not hurt you yet.[1] But you may have decided that to please Macbeth, you will offer me up like a weak, innocent lamb to be sacrificed.

Macduff. I am not a traitor.

Malcolm. But Macbeth is. A good person may do bad things if a king commands it. But I ask your pardon. I cannot know if you are good or bad. Angels are still bright, though the brightest fell.[2] Even if evil looks like good, good must still look like good.

Macduff. I have lost my hope.

Malcolm. Perhaps you lost it where I found my doubts. Why did you leave your wife and children, all you love, in that dangerous place without even saying good-bye? I beg you, don't let my suspicions hurt you. My suspicions are for my own safety. You may be perfectly trust-worthy, whatever I think.

Macduff. Bleed, bleed, poor country! Great tyranny, you are safe because goodness dares not stop

[1] At this point neither Macduff nor Malcolm know that Macbeth has murdered Macduff's family.

[2] Lucifer, the brightest angel, was thrown out of heaven for fighting against God, and became the devil. Macbeth, the best general, fought against his ruler.

you. Suffer under the wrongs that Macbeth does. He is the king now. [*To* Malcolm] Farewell, lord. I would not be the villain you think I am for all that the tyrant has and all of the rich East[3] with it.

Malcolm. Don't be offended. I don't completely mistrust you. I think our country is in great trouble. It weeps, it bleeds, and each day a cut is added to its wounds. I also think there would be people willing to help Scotland. The good king of England has offered thousands of soldiers to help. But for all of this, when I defeat Macbeth, cut off his head and hold it up on my sword, my poor country shall have more problems than it had before. It shall suffer more, and in more ways than ever, because of the next king after Macbeth.

Macduff. Who shall he be?

Malcolm. Me. I know all my own evils, and when they are looked at, evil Macbeth will seem as pure as snow. The country will think Macbeth a lamb compared with my unlimited evils.[4]

---

[3] the rich East—China, the Spice Islands, and India. At this time great wealth was coming out of these countries and into Europe.

[4] Malcolm is testing Macduff by describing himself as having many faults. If Macduff wants a better king, he will not accept the deeply flawed Malcolm as he describes himself. On the other hand, if Macduff simply wants Malcolm to come to Scotland so that Macbeth can have him killed, Macduff will not care how bad Malcolm is.

Macduff. Not from the armies of horrid hell can come a devil who is more evil than Macbeth.

Malcolm. I know that Macbeth is a murderer. He is greedy, **lecherous,**[5] false, tricky, violent, cruel. He has every sin that has a name. But, for instance, there is no end to my desires. I will want your wives, your daughters, your dignified older women, and your young girls. They will not fill up my desires. I would break all moral laws to get what I wanted. It's better to have Macbeth as king than to have me rule.

Macduff. Being ruled by such sexual desires is like being ruled by a tyrant. Such desires have destroyed kings. But do not fear, still you could be the king. You may have all the women you want. There will be plenty of willing women who will come to you because you are the king.[6]

Malcolm. Besides this, I have an unlimited need for wealth. If I were king, I would take the nobles' land, want one man's jewels, and another man's house. The more I took, the more I would want. I would destroy good and loyal men for their wealth.

---

[5] **lecherous**—too much concerned with sex.

[6] Macduff just failed Malcolm's test. Malcolm will try again.

Macduff. This greed is worse and bothers me more than youthful lust. Many kings have died for being too greedy. But do not fear, still you could be king. The property of the king is rich enough to satisfy you. We can take these vices if we get your goodness as well.

Malcolm. But I have no goodness. The kingly virtues, such as justice, truth, control, stability, generosity, mercy, humility, devotion, patience, courage, I do not like. I commit sin after sin, in many different ways. No, if I had the power, I should pour the sweet milk of agreement into hell, destroy all peace, ruin all unity on earth.

Macduff. O Scotland, Scotland!

Malcolm. If you think someone like me should rule Scotland, speak. I am as I have spoken.

Macduff. Fit to rule Scotland? You're not fit to live. O miserable nation, a bloody, tyrant thief rules you. When will Scotland see good days again? The man who should be king by his own words says he is unfit and shames his family. Your royal father was almost a saint. The queen, your mother, prayed on her knees more than she walked. She followed her religion faithfully every day of her life. Fare you well. These evils that you tell about yourself have banished me from Scotland. My hope ends here.[7]

Malcolm. Macduff, your noble anger shows you are not here to trick me and has wiped away my doubts about your truth and honor. Devilish Macbeth has tried to trick me by sending men to say what you have said. I had to be careful. But God above protect me because I will now do what you say. I lied about my faults. I would never do those evils. I have never been with a woman, scarcely want what is mine, have never broken my promise, would not betray even the worst man, and have never lied until I lied to you about myself. What I am truly is yours and my poor country's. I will do what you say.[8] Before you arrived, the English general Siward and ten thousand soldiers were ready to leave for Scotland. Now we'll go together, and may our chance at winning be as good as our cause is right. Why are you silent?

Macduff. Such welcome and unwelcome things at once. It's hard to make sense of all this.

---

[7] Macduff passed Malcolm's test. Now Malcolm must quickly make Macduff understand that the bad things he said about himself were not true.

[8] Malcolm will do what Macduff says because Malcolm is still young and very inexperienced. He hasn't led troops.

[*Enter a* Doctor.]

Malcolm. Well, we will speak more soon. [*To the* Doctor] Is the king[9] joining us soon?

Doctor. Yes, sir. Many sick people wait for his help. Medicine cannot help them, but God has given such holiness to the king of England that when he touches the sick, they are immediately well.

Malcolm. I thank you, doctor.

[*The* Doctor *exits.*]

Macduff. What disease is he talking about?

Malcolm. It's called "the evil." I have seen this good king cure people. How he gets heaven to help, only he knows. But people who have this strange sickness, who are all swollen with ulcers, look pitiful, and cannot be helped by doctors, he cures. He hangs a gold coin around their necks and prays. It is said he leaves this power to all the kings of England who come after him. He also can tell the future. God has given him other special powers as well.

---

[9] the king—Edward the Confessor. The king of England was very religious. The scene that follows has nothing to do with the play. But James I was the king of England, and Shakespeare put this scene in to flatter him.

[*Enter* Ross.]

Macduff. Look who is here.

Malcolm. He is from Scotland, but I don't know him.

Macduff. My ever-gentle cousin, welcome.

Malcolm. I know him now. I pray that God quickly removes what makes us strangers!

Ross. Sir, amen.[10]

Macduff. Is Scotland still the same?

Ross. Alas, poor country. It is a country almost afraid to know itself. Scotland can no longer be called our mother. Now it is our grave, where the only people who smile are those who don't know anything, where sighs and groans and shrieks are so common that no one notices them, where violent sorrow is the only strong emotion. No one asks who died when the church bell rings for a funeral, and good men's lives are over before the flowers they pick are wilted. They die before they get sick.

Macduff. O story too accurate and too true!

Malcolm. What's the newest grief?

---

[10] Used at the end of prayers. "Amen" can also mean "I agree with what was said" or "Me, too."

Ross. Every hour brings a new grief. Each minute brings a new grief.

Macduff. How is my wife?

Ross. Why, she is well.[11]

Macduff. And all my children?

Ross. Well too.

Macduff. The tyrant has not ruined their peace?

Ross. No, they were at peace when I left them.

Macduff. Don't be stingy in your speech. How is it?

Ross. When I came here to bring some news that I sadly carry, many good men were fighting against Macbeth. I saw them, and I saw the tyrant's army hunting them. Now is the time to help Scotland. If you were in Scotland, men would join you to fight against Macbeth. Our women would fight to get rid of their sorrow.

Malcolm. Let them be comforted. We are going there. The king of England has lent us good

---

[11] Ross says that Lady Macduff is well even though she's dead. Perhaps he can't bring himself to tell this terrible news. Perhaps he thinks it is better to give his political message first. These men are Christians. From a Christian point of view, Lady Macduff is well: she is at peace with God. This is a very common theme for Shakespeare.

Siward and ten thousand men; there isn't a more experienced or better soldier in any Christian country.

Ross. I wish I could answer this comfort with comfort for you. But I have words that should be howled out in the desert where no one would hear them.

Macduff. Who do they concern? Everyone or one person?

Ross. All good people share this sadness, though the main part is for you alone.

Macduff. If it is mine, don't keep it from me. Quickly tell me.

Ross. Don't hate me forever when I tell you the worst thing you have ever heard.

Macduff. Oh! I guess at it.

Ross. Your castle has been attacked without warning, your wife and babies savagely killed. To tell you how these innocents were killed would kill you.

Malcolm. Merciful heavens! Don't just be sad, give your sorrow words. If you don't let your grief come out, your heart will break.

Macduff. [Macduff *is in shock. He cannot understand or believe what has happened.*] My children too?

Ross. Wife, children, servants, everyone that could be found.

Macduff. Why wasn't I there? My wife killed too?

Ross. Just as I said.

Malcolm. Be comforted. Let's use revenge for medicine to cure this deadly grief.

Macduff. All my pretty ones? Did you say "all"? O hell-kite![12] All? What, all my pretty chickens and their mother with one fell[13] swoop?

Malcolm. Fight this like a man.

Macduff. I shall do so, but I must also feel it as a man. I cannot help remembering such things that were most precious to me. How could God let this happen? Sinful Macduff, they were all killed for me. Wicked man that I am, they were killed not because of their own actions, but for mine. Heaven give them rest now.

Malcolm. Let this sharpen your sword. Let your grief turn to anger. Don't hide your heart's feelings; turn them to rage.

---

[12] hell-kite—evil bird of prey, a type of hawk.
[13] fell—terrible.

Macduff. O I could cry like a woman and brag about revenge! But gentle heaven, don't waste my time! Bring me face to face with this fiend Macbeth. Put him within the reach of my sword. If he escapes me, let heaven forgive him.

Malcolm. This is a man's song. Come, let's go to the king of England. Our army is ready. We have everything except the king's permission to leave. Macbeth is ripe for shaking. We will be God's tools to destroy this evil man. Receive what comfort you may. The night is long that never turns to day.

[*They exit.*]

active

ACT FIVE, SCENE ONE

In a room in Macbeth's castle on Dunsinane Hill, a doctor and a lady who attends Lady Macbeth watch as she walks in her sleep and relives all the murders.

[*Enter a* Lady *and a* Doctor.]

Doctor. I have watched with you for two nights and have not seen her sleepwalk. When did she last walk?

Lady. Since his majesty started to fight. I have seen her get up from her bed, put on her robe, unlock her desk, take out paper, fold it, write on it, read it, seal it, and return to bed; yet all this time she was fast asleep.

Doctor. A great upset in nature, to get the good of sleep and still do things. In this upset sleep, besides walking and doing things, what have you heard her say?

Lady. That, sir, which I will not say.[1]

Doctor. You may tell me. It is right to tell a doctor.

Lady. I won't tell you or anyone, having no witness to say I told the truth.

[*Enter* Lady Macbeth *in sleeping clothes, carrying a candle.*]

Lady. Look, here she comes. This is what she usually does, and upon my life, she is asleep. Look at her; stand close.

Doctor. How did she get that candle?

Lady. Why, it was beside her. She always has light beside her.[2] It's her command.

[Lady Macbeth *starts rubbing her hands together. She is trying to rub the blood or guilt off.*]

Doctor. Her eyes are open.

Lady. Yes, but she is asleep.

Doctor. What is she doing? Look how she rubs her hands together.

Lady. She does this often. She seems to be washing her hands. I have known her to do this for a quarter of an hour.

---

[1] The lady has heard Lady Macbeth confess to the murders.

[2] At the beginning of the play, Lady Macbeth wanted to be in the dark, so no one could see the evil she was doing. Now she wishes to have light beside her at all times.

Lady Macbeth. [*Talking in her sleep*] Yet here's a spot.

Doctor. Hark, she speaks. I will write down what she says, to help me remember.

Lady Macbeth. Out, damned spot, out, I say! One. Two. Why then, it's time to do it. Hell is murky.[3] Fie, my lord, fie, a soldier and afraid? Why should we fear who knows it when no one can punish us because we are too powerful? Yet who would have thought the old man would have had so much blood in him?

Doctor. Did you hear that?

Lady Macbeth. The thane of Fife had a wife. Where is she now? What, will these hands never be clean? No more of that, my lord, no more of that. You ruin everything by acting this way.

Doctor. [*To the* Lady] Go to, go to. You have known what you should not know.

Lady. She has said what she should not say, I am sure of that. Heaven knows what she has known.

---

[3] murky—dark and gloomy. Lady Macbeth has gone mad. Next she speaks as if Macbeth were there.

Lady Macbeth. Here's the smell of blood still. All the perfumes of Arabia will not sweeten this little hand. [*She sighs*] Oh, Oh, Oh!

Doctor. What a terrible sigh! Her heart carries a heavy weight.

Lady. I would not have such a heart in my body even if I could be the queen.

Doctor. Well, well, well.

Lady. I pray God it be well, sir.

Doctor. This illness is beyond my skill. Yet, I have known people who walked in their sleep and died in their beds as good people.

Lady Macbeth. Wash your hands. Put on your robe. Look not so pale. I tell you again, Banquo's buried; he cannot come out of his grave.

Doctor. So, that's what happened.

Lady Macbeth. To bed, to bed. There's knocking at the gate. Come, come, come, come. Give me your hand. What's done cannot be undone. To bed, to bed, to bed.

[Lady Macbeth *exits.*]

Doctor. Will she go to bed now?

Lady. Right away.

Doctor. Terrible stories are being whispered. Unnatural actions make unnatural troubles. Sick minds will sometimes tell their troubles to their pillows. She needs a priest more than she needs a doctor. God, God forgive us all. Look after her. Take away anything she can use to hurt herself, but still watch her. So, goodnight. She has confused and amazed me. I know things now that I dare not talk about.

Lady. Good night, good doctor.

[*They exit.*]

Near Dunsinane, the Scottish leaders of the rebellion against Macbeth approach Birnam Wood. They are to join up with Malcolm, Macduff, Siward (the general sent by the king of England), and the English army.

[*Drums and flags. Enter* Menteith, Caithness, Angus, Lennox, *and Scottish* Soldiers.]

Menteith. The English army is near, led by Malcolm, his uncle Siward,[1] and the good Macduff. Revenge burns in them. The things Macbeth has done to them would cause dead men to rise up and help them.

Angus. We will meet them near Birnam Wood. They are coming that way.

Caithness. Is Donalbain with his older brother?

---

[1] In history, Malcolm was the nephew of the English general Siward.

Lennox. I know for certain, sir, that he is not with them. I have a list of those who fight with him. There is Siward's son and many inexperienced young men who have just become soldiers.

Menteith. What is the tyrant Macbeth doing?

Caithness. He strongly defends his castle on Dunsinane Hill. Some say he is mad; some who hate him less call it brave fury. His rule is so fat with evil that he cannot buckle the belt of righteous law around it.

Angus. Now does he feel his secret murders sticking on his hands. Every minute someone turns against him as he turned against Duncan. Those who stay with him only obey him because they are afraid, not because they wish to follow him. His title of king is too big for him. He is like a dwarf wearing a giant's clothing.

Menteith. Who can blame him that his troubled thoughts are bothering him when all that is within him **condemns**[2] itself for being there?

Caithness. Well, let's march on to meet with our true king. He will be the medicine that will cure this sick country, and with him we will pour

---

[2] **condemns**—strongly disapproves of.

out every drop of our blood to make our country well.[3]

Lennox. We will give as much blood as is needed to water the true flower and drown the weeds.[4] Let's march to Birnam Wood.

[*They exit marching, ready for battle.*]

---

[3] Doctors often bled people. They cut the person and let the "bad" blood out. The Scottish soldiers are willing to bleed so they can free their country from Macbeth's rule.

[4] The true flower (the king) would be Malcolm; the weed would be Macbeth.

In the castle on Dunsinane Hill, Macbeth believes himself safe because of the witches' predictions. A servant tells Macbeth the English army is near. Macbeth gets ready to fight. The doctor says medicine cannot help Lady Macbeth; she should be watched.

[*Enter* Macbeth, *the* Doctor, *and* Attendants.]

Macbeth. Don't bring me any more reports. Let the deserting thanes flee. What do I care? Until Birnam Wood moves to Dunsinane, I don't need to fear because nothing can defeat me. And, who is this boy Malcolm? Didn't a woman give him birth? The apparitions told me that no man born of woman shall ever have power over me. Then leave me, false thanes, and go to the weak, luxury-loving English. My mind and my heart shall never sag with doubt nor shake with fear.

[*A* Servant *enters, obviously upset and afraid.*]

Macbeth. The devil turn you black, you white-faced, cowardly fool. What makes you look like a stupid goose?

Servant. There are ten thousand—[*He cannot speak.*]

Macbeth. Geese, villain?

Servant. Soldiers, sir.

Macbeth. Go pinch your cheeks and make them red, you lily-livered boy. What soldiers, fool? Death of your soul! Your linen-white cheeks show you are afraid. What soldiers, whey-face?[1]

Servant. The English army, so please you.

Macbeth. Take your face out of here. [*The* Servant *exits.*] Seyton![2] [*To himself*] I am sick at heart when I see—Seyton, I say!—This fight will keep me on the throne as I wish or unseat me now. I have lived long enough. My way of life is dry and withered, like a yellow leaf. I do not expect to get what should go with old age. I will not have honor, love, obedience, and many friends, but in their place I will have curses, not

---

[1] whey-face—looking like thin, watery, sour milk.

[2] Seyton—an army officer who serves Macbeth, an aide-de-camp.

loud but deep, false honor, only breath which the poor heart would like to deny and dare not. —Seyton!

[*Enter* Seyton.]

Seyton. What's your gracious pleasure?

Macbeth. What is the news?

Seyton. The report is true, my lord.

Macbeth. I'll fight until my flesh is cut off my bones. Give me my armor.

Seyton. It's not needed yet.

Macbeth. I'll put it on. Send out more soldiers. Search the countryside. Hang anyone who talks of fear. Give me my armor. [*To the* Doctor] How is your patient, doctor?

Doctor. Not so sick, my lord, as she is troubled with many dreams that keep her from a healing sleep.

Macbeth. Cure her of that! Can't you heal a sick mind and pull from the memory a deep sorrow? Can't you burn out the troubles of the brain, and with some sweet medicine make the patient forget and clean out the stuff that weighs on the heart?

Doctor. The patient must help herself with those problems.

Macbeth. Throw medicine to the dogs.[3] I don't want it. [*To* Seyton] Come, help me put on my armor. [Servants *start to help* Macbeth *get ready for war.*] Give me my staff. Seyton, send out more men. [*To the* Doctor] Doctor, the thanes all leave me. If you could, Doctor, tell me what's wrong with my country, find her disease.[4] Wash it away until Scotland is strong and healthy. I would then applaud you and applaud you again. [*To the* Servants *helping him dress for war*] Pull it off, I say. [*To the* Doctor] What medicine or drug would clean these English out of Scotland? Have you heard about them?

Doctor. Yes, my good lord. We hear you getting ready for them.

Macbeth. [*To* Servants] Bring it after me. [*To himself, but everyone can hear*] I will not be afraid of death and ruin until Birnam Forest comes to Dunsinane.

---

[3] Macbeth means if medicine can't help mental/spiritual problems, it's not worth anything.

[4] The irony here is that Macbeth is what's wrong with the country. Of course, he can't see that.

Doctor. [*To himself*] If I were away from Dunsinane and clear, money should not again bring me here.

[*They exit.*]

Near Birnam Wood, the Scottish army has joined Malcolm,
Macduff, and Siward. Malcolm has the soldiers cut down
tree branches to hide themselves.

[*Drums and flags. Enter* Malcolm, Siward, Macduff,
Young Siward, Menteith, Caithness, Angus, *and*
Soldiers *marching for battle.*]

Malcolm. Cousins, I hope the days are near when
our homes will be safe.

Menteith. We know they are.

Siward. What wood is this?

Menteith. This is the wood of Birnam.

Malcolm. Tell every soldier to cut tree branches
and carry them in front of himself. That way we
shall hide ourselves, making it harder to tell
where we are and how many of us there are.

Soldier. It shall be done.

Siward. All we know is that the confident tyrant Macbeth is still in his castle on Dunsinane Hill. He does not try to stop us from laying siege[1] to it.

Malcolm. It's his main hope. Where people can, they have left him. No one serves him except those that are forced to, and they aren't loyal to him.

Macduff. Let us wait to judge until we see what happens. Now let's prepare to be good soldiers.

Siward. The time comes that will make us know what we actually have. We can guess what will happen, but we can't know until we fight; let us start this battle.

[*They exit marching.*]

---

[1] laying siege—surrounding a castle and not allowing food in until the people inside have to give up. Of course, the people outside might give up before the people inside do. Macbeth thinks he can last longer than the army outside.

In the castle, most of Macbeth's men have deserted him. Macbeth believes the castle is strong enough to protect him. He is told that Lady Macbeth is dead. A messenger says that Birnam Wood is moving toward the castle.

[*Enter* Macbeth, Seyton, *and* Soldiers, *with drums and flags.*]

Macbeth. Hang our banners on the outside wall. The cry is still "They come!" Our castle's strength will laugh at a siege. Let them stay out there until hunger and disease eat them up. If they didn't have men fighting with them that should be fighting on our side, we would have met them in battle, face to face, and beat them back to England.

[*The audience can hear women crying offstage.*]

Macbeth. What is that noise?

Seyton. It is the sound of women crying, my lord.

[Seyton *exits to see what has happened.*]

Macbeth. I have almost forgot the taste of fear. At one time I would have gone cold when I heard a cry in the night, and my hair would move as if it were alive at the sound of a terrible noise. I have eaten horrors until I am full of them. Terrible events don't bother me any more.

[*Enter* Seyton.]

Macbeth. What was that cry?

Seyton. The queen, my lord, is dead.

Macbeth. She should have died hereafter;
There would have been a time for such a word.
Tomorrow and tomorrow and tomorrow
Creeps in this petty pace from day to day
To the last syllable of recorded time,
And all our yesterdays have lighted fools
The way to dusty death. Out, out, brief candle!
Life's but a walking shadow, a poor player,[1]
That struts and frets his hour upon the stage

---

[1] shadow, a poor player—actor.

And then is heard no more. It is a tale
Told by an idiot, full of sound and fury,
Signifying nothing.[2]

[*A* Messenger *enters.*]

Messenger. Gracious my lord, I have to report
what I think I saw, but I don't know how to
tell you.

Macbeth. Well, say it, sir.

Messenger. As I stood watch on Dunsinane Hill, I
looked toward Birnam Wood, and soon I
thought the forest began to move.

Macbeth. Liar and villain!

Messenger. You are right to be angry with me if
I'm not telling the truth. Within three miles
of the castle you can see it coming. I saw a
moving forest.

Macbeth. If you are lying, I will hang you upon a
tree until you starve to death. If you are telling
the truth, I don't care if you do the same thing
to me. [*To himself*] I'm not so sure now. I begin
to doubt the fiends who tell the truth and yet

---

[2] This famous soliloquy is in Shakespeare's original words. The American
novelist William Faulkner used it as the outline for his novel *The Sound and
the Fury.*

tell a lie. They said, "Fear not until Birnam Wood comes to Dunsinane," and now a forest comes toward Dunsinane. [*To his men*] Arm, arm, and be ready to fight! [*To himself*] If what he says is true, I can neither run from here nor stay here. I begin to be weary of the sun, and wish the estate of the world were now undone.³ [*To the* Soldiers] Ring the alarm bell! [*To himself*] Blow wind, come ruin, at least we'll die fighting.

[*They exit.*]

---

³ the estate of the world were now undone—the settled order of the universe was destroyed.

Outside Macbeth's castle on Dunsinane Hill, the English and Scottish armies attack.

[*Drum and flags. Enter* Malcolm, Siward, Macduff, *and their army, carrying tree limbs.*][1]

Malcolm. We are near enough. Throw down your covering branches and show yourselves as soldiers. [*To* Siward *and his son,* Young Siward] You, worthy uncle, shall with my cousin, your noble son, lead the main part of our army. Worthy Macduff and we[2] shall do what is left to do.

---

[1] Many scenes in Act Five are very short. Act Five is exciting and colorful. The scenes go fast. The armies are preparing to fight. Cannons are fired in a special effects room above the theater. Groups of soldiers charge across the stage or fight in the background.

[2] Malcolm seems confident that he will be king. He is using the royal plural "we" instead of "I."

Siward. Fare you well. If we find the tyrant's army tonight, let us be beaten if we cannot fight.

Macduff. Make all our trumpets speak; sound them all, those loud messengers of blood and death.

[*They exit. The trumpets are blowing the signal to attack.*]

ACT FIVE, SCENE SEVEN

On the battlefield, Macbeth kills Young Siward. Macduff searches for Macbeth, and Malcolm's army takes the castle.

[*Enter* Macbeth.]

Macbeth. They have tied me to a stake. I cannot leave. But like a bear, I must fight until the end.[1] Who is he who was not born of woman? Such a one am I to fear, or none.

[*Enter* Young Siward, *the English general's son. This is his first battle.*]

Young Siward. What is your name?

Macbeth. You would be afraid to hear it.

---

[1] Bear baiting was a favorite entertainment. Bears would be chained to a ring or stake in the floor. Dogs would be allowed to attack them. Macbeth feels like one of these bears waiting to be attacked.

Young Siward. No, though you call yourself a hotter name than any in hell.

Macbeth. My name is Macbeth.

Young Siward. The devil himself could not say a name more hateful to my ears.

Macbeth. No, nor more fearful.

Young Siward. You lie, hated tyrant. With my sword I'll prove you lie.

[*They fight.* Macbeth *is by far the more experienced swordsman. It is an uneven fight. At the end,* Macbeth *kills* Young Siward.]

Macbeth. You were born of a woman. But swords I smile at, weapons I laugh at, if they are used by a man that is of woman born.

[Macbeth *exits.*]

[*The trumpets sound.* Macduff *enters. He is hunting for* Macbeth.]

Macduff. Over there is the greatest noise. Tyrant, show your face! If you are killed by someone else, my wife and children's ghosts will haunt me. I cannot fight these hired soldiers. Either you, Macbeth, or else I will not use this sword today. You should be over there. By all the noise, someone important is there. Let me find him, Fortune, and I'll never ask for anything else.

[*He exits.*]

[*Trumpets sound.* Malcolm *and* Siward *enter.*]

Siward. This way, my lord. The castle has been taken without a fight. Macbeth's people leave him so they can fight against him. The noble thanes have done bravely in the war. We have almost won. There isn't much left to do.

Malcolm. We have met with enemies that fight on our side.

Siward. Sir, enter the castle.

[*They exit. The trumpets sound.*]

At another part of the battlefield, Macbeth and Macduff fight. Macduff says he was not born of woman. Ross reports the death of Young Siward. Macduff enters with Macbeth's head and asks everyone to greet Malcolm as the new king.

[*Enter* Macbeth.]

Macbeth. Why should I play the Roman fool and die on my own sword?[1] While I see enemy soldiers alive, the cuts look better on them.

[*Enter* Macduff.]

Macduff. Turn, hellhound, turn!

Macbeth. Of all men, I have avoided you. But stay away. My soul is guilty of killing too many of yours already.

---

[1] A Roman general might kill himself if he lost a war. Shakespeare wrote about several Roman generals, including Julius Caesar.

Macduff. I have nothing to say to you; my voice is in my sword, you bloodier villain than words can say.

[*They fight.* Macduff *is experienced, but* Macbeth *is the better swordsman. It looks like* Macbeth *will kill* Macduff. *They pause.*]

Macbeth. You are wasting your time. It would be easier for you to make the air bleed than to hurt me. Let your sword fall on heads that can be hurt. I bear a charmed life. I cannot be killed by any man of woman born.

Macduff. Give up your charm, and let the evil spirit you have always served tell you that Macduff was from his mother's womb untimely ripped.[2]

Macbeth. Cursed be your tongue for telling me this. It has made me a coward! And be those lying witches no longer believed. They juggle the meaning of words to trick us. What they say, happens, but not what we had hoped from what they said. I'll not fight you.[3]

---

[2] Macduff was not born naturally. He was cut out of his mother in a Caesarian-section, which was named for Julius Caesar, who was delivered that way. The witches have tricked Macbeth again.

[3] Macbeth will not fight Macduff because he knows now that Macduff will kill him. The witches' predictions do come true.

Macduff. Then give up, coward, and live to be a show to be stared at. We'll put you in a cage like a strange monster and hang a sign that says "Here is the tyrant."[4]

Macbeth. I will not give up to kiss the ground before young Malcolm's feet and be attacked by the common people's curses. Though Birnam Wood comes to Dunsinane and you are not born of woman, yet I will fight to the end. Before my body I throw my warlike shield. Lay on, Macduff, and to hell with him that first cries "Stop! Enough!"

[*They exit fighting.*]

[*Drums and flags.* Malcolm, Siward, Ross, the Thanes, *and* Soldiers *enter.*]

Malcolm. I wish the friends who are missing would arrive safely.

Siward. Some must die; and yet by those I see here, so great a victory is cheaply won.

Malcolm. Macduff is missing, and your noble son.

---

[4] This is one of the most important turning points in the play. At this point Macbeth must make a great choice: to give up or fight on, even though he knows he will lose.

Ross. [*to* Siward] Your son, my lord, has paid a soldier's debt. He only lived till he was a man, and when he proved his manhood by doing his duty, like a man he died.

Siward. Then he is dead?

Ross. Yes, and carried off the field. Your sorrow must not be measured by his worth because then it has no end.

Siward. Was he wounded fighting or running away?

Ross. Fighting.

Siward. Why then, now he is God's soldier! If I had as many sons as I have hairs, I would not wish them a better death.

Malcolm. He's worth more sorrow, and I will grieve for him.

Siward. He's worth no more. They say he died well and did what he should have done. And so, God be with him. Here comes newer comfort.

[*Enter* Macduff *carrying Macbeth's head.*]

Macduff. Hail, king! For so you are. Look, here is the tyrant's head. Our country is free. I see you surrounded by the best men in the country, that speak my greeting in their minds. I ask them to speak aloud with me. Hail, king of Scotland!

[*Trumpets sound as everyone shouts "Hail, king of Scotland!"*]

Malcolm. I shall not take long to reward you all. My thanes and kinsmen, from now on you are earls, a title that Scotland has never had. You are the first to be so honored. There is much more to do. I must bring back our exiled friends who escaped the tyrant. I must punish the cruel followers of this dead butcher and his fiend-like queen. She, it is thought, killed herself. This and whatever needs to be done, by the grace of God, we will do. So thanks to all at once and to each one of you, whom we invite to see us crowned at Scone.

[*Trumpets, and all exit.*]

AFTERNOTE ABOUT THE WITCHES' PREDICTIONS

In the story of Macbeth, the witches make some announcements. Are they predictions?

When Macbeth first meets the witches, they greet him as the thane of Glamis, which he is, so that's not a prediction. Then they greet him as thane of Cawdor, which he is but doesn't know yet. The last greeting they give Macbeth is that he will be king in the future. That is a reasonable guess. When a Scottish king died, the thanes (the six or so most powerful men next to the king) voted for the next king, usually one of the thanes. Macbeth is already thane of Glamis and thane of Cawdor, so he has two votes. He has just saved his kingdom from invasion. He's a great hero, soldier, and general. He's Duncan's cousin. The king's sons are too young. Macbeth would be the choice of the thanes if Duncan died.

When Macbeth returns to the witches, he is told to "Beware Macduff" who finally kills him. Further, they say he will not be defeated until Birnam Wood comes to Dunsinane Hill. This happens when Malcolm's soldiers cut tree limbs down to use to hide themselves as they attack.

The other prediction is that Macbeth cannot be defeated by any man born of woman. Macduff was not "born." He was cut out of his mother before he had a chance to be born in a Caesarean-section delivery.

The witches are asked whether Banquo's children will be kings. The witches say yes. But Banquo's children do not become kings in the play. It's another of the witches' jokes. Seven generations later, Banquo and Fleance's descendants marry into the royal family, Malcolm's descendants. So Banquo's descendants become kings of Scotland. About eight generations later, one of his descendants is James VI of Scotland, who becomes James I of England, the king who paid Shakespeare to write *Macbeth*. So, in the end, all of the witches' predictions come true.